From Grief to Glory

A memoir and guide to finding joy after loss

Alisa Latty – Alleyne

ISBN: 9798394947858
Imprint: Independently published

The greatest gift I have ever known is having the Lord open my eyes to a whole new chapter of my story. I give Him all the praise as He has brought me 'From Grief to Glory.'

I dedicate this book to the strength and love of my new husband Carlyle, my son Jacob and all my family, both past and present, for your unwavering support. This book is a tribute honouring the memory of my late husband, Clive Clarence Alexis Harewood. It is also a celebration of the resilience of the human spirit, the power of love to endure and a reflection of the hope that lies ahead.

A Note from The Author

I wanted to take a moment to personally thank you for choosing my book. I hope that it offers you comfort, hope, and encouragement as you navigate your own grief journey or gain insights into how to help others who have. Losing someone close to us can be incredibly difficult, and it's a journey that no one should have to go through alone.

As you read through my memoir, please know that my intention is to provide you with a quick and easy read that you can refer to at various stages of your journey through grief. I hope that my story and the lessons I have learned will resonate with you and help you move through the different stages of grief and come out on the other side.

As the author of this book, it is incredibly important to me that my words are accessible and meaningful to readers from all walks of life. While my own faith in Jesus has played an integral role in my own journey through grief, I recognise that not everyone shares those same beliefs. My intention is not to convert or persuade, but rather to offer my own story and the insights that have come from it. I firmly believe that the lessons I have learned along the way are applicable to anyone, regardless of their religious or spiritual background. Ultimately, this book is about the universal experience of grief and the complex emotions that accompany it. I hope that my personal experiences will resonate with you, and that the understandings I have gained will prove valuable, no matter what your beliefs may be.

I want to thank you in advance for taking the time to read my book, and I hope that it provides you with some comfort and solace during this difficult time.

With blessing and love,

Alisa x

ACKNOWLEDGMENTS

First and foremost, I want to express my gratitude to my son Jacob. Throughout our journey together, you have been my constant source of support and love. I want you to know how much I appreciate all the times you sacrificed your time with me so that I could focus on my mission to make the world a better place. You never once complained, and that means more to me than you will ever know. I'm so proud of the incredible young man you have become. Your curiosity and desire to understand the meaning of life inspire me every day to continue on my own journey of discovery. I cannot wait to see all the amazing things you will accomplish in your life. Mummy loves you more more more.

My darling Carlyle, you have a way of making me feel like I am unstoppable, like I can be anyone, do anything, and go anywhere. I thank God every day for bringing you into my life. You are not just my husband, but my best friend, my confidant, my coach, and my love. It is an honour to be able to call you mine. Together, we can take on anything that the world throws our way. Let's do this baby!

To my mother, I have to pause to try and think of all the things to say to you and none of them seem big enough to express the love that I have for you. You are an incredibly strong, determined, and loving mother who always puts her family first. I am so proud of everything you have accomplished, from raising a troubled teen to the successful person I am today. This book is not just a personal achievement, but a testament to your constant support and encouragement. Keep seeking God, stay happy, and know that there is always light at the end of the tunnel.

To my dad's Harvey and Eddie, I see a mixture of your work ethics, humility, comedic timing, and love of music in myself in different measures. Thank you for always encouraging me to never give up on my dreams and for being such wonderful role models of what a man is capable of.

To Syble, my stepmother, I am so grateful for your spiritual guidance. Your prayers and congratulations on my achievements mean so much to me, and I feel truly blessed to have you in my life.

To Jackie, you are not just a big sister, but also a source of inspiration and encouragement. I am grateful for the fact that our relationship and friendship have flourished over the years. Your honesty and willingness to tell me the truth, even when it is difficult for me to hear, is a testament to what a true big sister should be. Thank you for everything that you do.

To Machaela, thank you for the support you provided, especially during those first four weeks. You were always there by my side, offering a listening ear or simply being present in silence. The sacrifices you made to be with me will never be forgotten, and I am forever grateful for your selflessness. Our relationship is truly special, and I know that you would do it all again in a heartbeat. Thank you for everything.

To Jonell, thank you for being my pillar of strength during those trying years after his passing. Your home was my haven where I could come, hand over Jacob to you and grieve without any judgment or expectations. You allowed me the space to just be, and I cannot thank you enough for that. Your kitchen table will forever hold a special place in my heart as it was our sacred place where we shared our deepest emotions. Your unyielding support and care carried me through even when I was in denial of not being okay. I am truly grateful for your presence in my life and cherish the bond we share. Thank you for being my safe space.

To Kama, you may not have thought that you did much, but you did more than you know. Always there if I needed you and always there to make me laugh. To see you grow up has been one of the great privileges of my life so far, you are a beauty inside and out, thank you.

To Auntie Tessel, I admire and appreciate you. Your love and encouragement have been a guiding light in my life, and your example of strength and resilience has helped me see my own value and worth. I love you so much, and I feel lucky to have you in my life. And to Uncle David, I will always be grateful for the time you spent with me and Jacob after Benny's passing. Your presence and kind words helped me through one of the toughest moments of my life, and I will never forget the encouragement you gave me. Thank you for always being there for me.

To Monica, you will forever be my mother. You showed me what true humility is. To Clarence my dad, Tammy and Tia my sisters, Caroline for the coconut water, Dia and all my BIM family, you will always be family.

To my closest friends who have been there for me during my darkest moments, thank you for picking me up off the floor and providing me with a safe haven free from judgment. Rachel, your heart is pure gold, and you never hesitate to go above and beyond for those you love. We've been friends since primary school, and I'll still beat you in a 100-meter sprint! Sherena, we've been through it all together and I couldn't ask for a better ride or die. And to Krissie, I may have met you later in my journey, but I feel so blessed to have you in my life. You are a true friend, kind-hearted and humble. Thank you all for being my sisters and best friends for life.

To the incredible individuals who were there for me during a challenging time. Claudia, Elizabeth, Denise, Tyrone, Mary, Tom, Kevin, Warren, Kham, and my beloved friend Rebecca, who has since passed away, formed my first responder team and went above and beyond to aid me during those crucial first four weeks. Your generosity, compassion, and support will forever be remembered and cherished. Thank you all from the bottom of my heart.

To Sean and Rach from Polywood Studios for your hard work and guidance during the creation of my book, From Grief to Glory. Your expertise in copy editing and graphic design was invaluable, and I am truly grateful for your unflinching commitment to making this book the best it could be. Your honesty, creativity, and respect for my vision were evident in every step of the process, and I couldn't have asked for better partners in this endeavour. Thank you for being the creative geniuses that you are, and for helping me bring this project to life.

Thank you to all the beta readers your dedication to reading and reviewing every chapter, while providing honest and heartfelt feedback, truly made a difference in the final product. Your suggestions and revisions challenged me to become a better writer and ensured that the book was the best it could be. I appreciate your time, effort, and support more than words can express.

Trying to fit the names of all the people who helped me on my journey from Grief to Glory into a couple of pages is impossible. So, I'm going to ask for forgiveness in advance for anybody that I have not named individually. Thank you for your unconditional love, friendship, listening ear or in whatever way you helped me; I will never forget your contribution to my life story, and I thank you from the bottom of my heart to the depths of my soul.

CONTENTS

INTRODUCTION

My life was very different at the start of 2015, I felt like I was living the dream. I had an incredible husband, a son I adored and a wonderfully supportive family. I was living a very comfortable, materialistic life in the affluent suburbs of Northville, Michigan, in the USA. Working for a global engineering organisation, and driven by my need to succeed, I had become the first woman to run a $30million sales and delivery function in the company's history. My position rewarded me with a six-figure salary which gave me a home by the lake, a Range Rover, my son in a private nursery, an extensive array of clothes and shoes. It was safe to say that I had a lot of STUFF. Then, one morning, on the 14th of April 2015, my life changed forever.

Have you ever woken up in the morning feeling like life could not get any better? Well, that is how I felt as I kissed my husband goodbye, not knowing that it would be the last time I would see him alive again. We were just four years into our marriage when he tragically and suddenly passed away. For those that have experienced loss, you will know that the grief process is brutally painful. I had no idea how I would survive without him by my side. How was I going to raise my son as a single parent? How would I be able to continue my career without his support and guidance? If I couldn't work at a senior level, how could I afford the lifestyle I had created for us. So many questions, fears and anxieties about the future. So much pain to wade through. Where could I find some help to try and prepare me for all of this? I searched high and low for books and resources that could help me try and understand what journey I was about to go on, and to be honest, I drew a blank every time. There seemed to be little to no support groups for young widows or children who had lost parents. The books and resources I found seemed to focus on explaining nothing other than the stages of grief:

- Denial
- Anger
- Bargaining
- Depression
- Acceptance

All of the places I looked to for help seemed to sugarcoat the reality that this journey would be a fight for my very survival. So when making the decision to write this book, I wanted to open up all the deep wounds and write from a place of raw authenticity. As a result, nothing in this book has been diluted or edited out.

During my grief, I took comfort in many unhealthy things. I left my job and ultimately my career and moved back to the UK to start an uncertain new life. I became dependant on sex, alcohol and marijuana to numb my pain and fill the void. My anger at how my life had been obliterated in one day grew into tensions with my family and strained many friendships, some of which have never recovered. The grip and stronghold of loneliness, anxiety and depression led me to suicidal thoughts and ultimately a mental breakdown.

During many seasons of my grief, one thing that kept bringing me back to a place of peace was my decision to follow Jesus and become a Christian. The journey that the

Lord took me on has been the biggest test of faith and endurance I have faced in my 45 years of being on this earth. But Jesus has and continues to show up for me. Every time the devil tries to tell me I can't, Jesus tells me I can. He chose me for this assignment and brought me through all of this so that I can be here to share my story with you and let you know that there is hope through loss; that a new purpose and a new life is waiting for you. Grief and loss will change you, that is inevitable, but it does not have to define you for the rest of your life.

If you are not a believer, then that's absolutely okay, and I am not here to judge you for that. I am not here to change your mind or convert you either; that's not my job. My role is to simply tell you that I was one way, and now I am completely different, and the thing that happened in between was Jesus. He replaced all the things that were leading to my long-term destruction with his presence. My relationship with Him has become the most amazing transformation of my life to date.

If you are at the start of, stuck in or travelling through grief, I want to tell you that as dark as it may seem right now, there is hope. As you read on, you will hear the real story of darkness that came from me losing the person I loved. A story of how trusting in Jesus didn't take away the immediate pain; in fact, I went through more turmoil than words cannot describe. But it did give me the belief that things could and will continue to get better if I trusted Him. I hope it teaches you some of the vital lessons I learned on the way and guides you to the place where the world will feel like it is spinning in sync again. So, continue reading and let me show you how my life has been changed by renewing my mind, healing my broken heart but most significantly, let me show you how I have gone from grief to glory.

CHAPTER 1

I SHOULD HAVE REMEMBERED MY COAT

By April 2015, Benny, our son Jacob, and I had been living in Michigan for almost four years. We had moved from the West Midlands in the UK for my international promotion when our son was just two years old. One of the many things that Benny loved in life was sports, from the camaraderie of team sports like football to the intensity of a singular sport like athletics, where your performance is on show for all to see. In the summer of 2010, before Jacob was born, I took him to see his beloved Chelsea football stadium for a tour of the grounds. It was like watching a child open their gifts at Christmas, as he experienced the enormity of being in the changing rooms where iconic players had prepared for games; to standing in the tunnel getting ready to head to the football field, his grin from ear to ear was priceless. Moving to the USA meant we could experience firsthand the iconic American sports, but due to my busy work schedule, we had only had time to watch American football on TV or at a sports bar, and we had not seen a baseball or basketball game together.

On the Friday before my late husband Benny died, we decided to see a basketball game and went to see the Detroit

Pistons play at the Auburn Hills arena. It had been such a great family night, full of new experiences, fun, and loud shouts of "Defence" over and over again. When we left the arena around 9 pm, the weather had turned from an early April afternoon spring warmth to a colder nighttime drizzle. As usual, I had forgotten my coat. True to Benny's caring and protective nature, he took off his jacket and placed it around my shoulders to shield me from the chilly night air. These simple yet powerful gestures were one of the things that I loved most about him. Take the first gift he ever gave me as an example. I had expressed a desire at some point to buy a really nice jewellery box. I hadn't selected one, and it wasn't on the top of my to-do list to purchase. But true to form, a couple of months later, he didn't just go out and buy me an expensive one; he put careful thought into it, gathered all the raw materials he would need, took his time, and made me one by hand. He would often write love notes and leave them in the fridge next to a packed lunch that he would have prepared for me. I can't remember a day that he saw me and didn't tell me that I looked beautiful, and without fail, when he walked through our front door after his day at work, he would kiss me and say, "hello, baby."

After he died, I internalised the night he gave me his jacket and punished myself, replaying the should-have, would-have, could-have moments on a loop. The significance of that particular gesture on that specific night is incomparable to any other. It would prove to be one act of kindness I wish he had never done, and the one night I wish I had remembered my coat.

An Enemy Called Asthma

Over the days that followed our family's Friday night out, Benny developed a cold that later turned into flu-like symptoms. This resulted in him taking two very out-of-character sick days from work. On Tuesday morning, he booked an emergency appointment and headed to the doctor to ensure that everything was okay. You might think that it was a bit extreme, but if you suffered from chronic, acute asthma, like Benny, and one of your asthmatic triggers was getting a cold, which had seen him hospitalised on several previous occasions, it was necessary. The most severe of those hospitalisations occurred after he had returned to Barbados from visiting me in December 2008. On New Year's Day of 2009, his asthma attack had resulted in a collapsed lung, and he spent five days in an induced coma. His family and friends were at the hospital day and night, waiting to see what would happen when or even if he woke up. I made copious amounts of phone calls to his strong and kind-hearted mother in Barbados for what felt like hourly check-ins. After a particular conversation with her, I caught an emergency flight out that could not have been timed more perfectly. The day I arrived; it was like a fairy tale. He was brought out of his coma, woke up, and went on to make an incredible recovery. Benny left the hospital three days later and asked me to marry him, all of which happened in the space of seven days. I remember his mum telling me that she had written his eulogy during this time as she didn't think he would make it. We went on to have seven more years together before she would end up having to read it.

Benny and I had very differing opinions about how he should manage his asthma. He always opted for natural remedies, while I always looked at what could be done medically. Nutrition and fitness were key priorities in his life. I always joked that the gym was the third person in our marriage. I secretly admired his determination to live his life without borders, never allowing his illness to disable him. I certainly loved how his body looked, as a result of his dedication to lifting weights; he was gorgeous. However, some accompanying issues walked hand in hand with his asthma that no amount of fitness or nutrition could resolve. He could not taste or smell anything at all. He had sleep apnea, which disrupted his regular sleep pattern, resulting in him being exhausted at the end of every day. He had severe nasal polyps, which meant he had trouble breathing through his nose, causing continuous nasal drippage. I took him to several asthma consultants and Ears, Nose & Throat specialists in both the UK and the US, all of whom would advise additional medical solutions, strangling his desire to be medication-free. After many attempts to find solutions to his illness, in 2013, we had a significant test of our marriage. Arguments were like buses; one came, then more followed in rapid succession. They all centred around our differing views on treatment. After one particularly big argument - the mother of all rows - I was told in no uncertain terms to stay out of it; it was his body, his illness, and his decision!

After he died, I remember sorting through his paperwork and finding that several months before, his doctor had prescribed him tablets that are used as long-term therapy for some people with severe asthma. I found these tablets half used in our medicine cabinet when I was packing up to move back to the UK at the end of 2015. He had clearly made a unilateral decision to not take a tablet every day. I also found prescription receipts that showed he had been collecting a new rescue inhaler on average every couple of months for over a year. You put the two of these together, and the result is that his asthma was conclusively not under control. Were these contributing factors to his death? I'll never know. But to say that I wish I had dug my heels in more and insisted that he continued with my course of action would be an understatement. Ultimately though, he was right. It was his asthma, and he wanted to fight it his way; I just wish the outcome had been much, much different.

Date: Tuesday The 14th Of April 2014| 20:30 And 22:30

It was about 8:30 pm when I arrived home with Jacob that evening to find that Benny had still not returned from his doctor's appointment in the afternoon. I found it a little strange that he hadn't come home yet but didn't overthink it. You have to remember this was not our first rodeo; his doctor's appointment had been at around 6 pm, and I knew the 'normal' drill. I told myself they must have put him on a nebuliser at the surgery, and after that, he would have made his way to collect his prescription from the pharmacy. It was also well past Jacob's bedtime, so I rushed around getting him washed and dressed for bed whilst calling Benny's phone at 10-minute intervals. Jacob fell asleep at 9:15 pm, by which time my calmness had quickly turned into anxiety as I continued to call his phone over and over. Every time I heard the answering machine message, the nauseous feeling in the pit of my stomach grew into a deeper and deeper ache of uncertainty. Where was he? Why wasn't he answering!

At 10:00 pm, it was now entirely out of character for him not to have called or sent a message to say where he was. He couldn't have popped in to visit family as we had none where we were, and our friend circle was also tiny. We did, however, have one couple that we'd created a special bond with, and I had a glimmer of hope that he might be there. I called to find out if Benny was with them; when they said no, my anxiety and deep ache immediately grew to panic. Just as I was about to call his phone for the 12th time, my phone started ringing from an unknown number.

Date: Tuesday The 14th Of April 2014 | 22:30 - 00:00

After confirming my details, all the lady at the end of my phone could tell me was that my husband was at the hospital. He couldn't speak, and I needed to come. I can't recall what happened in the hour following that call. Other than when I arrived at the hospital, a man sitting at reception took my details, picked up his desk phone, made a call, and then guided me to a little room. Have you ever experienced a short wait that felt like it was longer than it was? Well, I waited in that room for no more than ten minutes, but it felt like a decade. My leg could not stop shaking! I remember sitting alone thinking, whatever it is, please let it be manageable. Three people then entered the room, and I knew it was not going to be good news from the look on their faces. As I read their name badges, I knew I was being greeted by a doctor, a nurse, and a chaplain. The chaplain was a tall and kind-looking man with brown hair and glasses. He came into the room last, and as I realised the severity of his presence, my body went cold. Before anyone could say a word and scared by his presence, I said very sternly,' what is the chaplain doing here?'

Everything that came next was white noise. I hadn't fainted or anything, but I did feel like I'd disappeared, hearing and seeing nothing. The doctor began explaining what had happened. Through the crackling invisibility of the moment and with a nervous reluctance in her voice, she said that Benny had been brought in from the doctor's surgery by the paramedics because of complications with his asthma. The paramedics had called ahead to explain the emergency, and when he arrived at the hospital just after 8:30 pm, he had been struggling to breathe and was combative. They immediately sedated him, intubated him, and put him on a ventilator to assist his breathing. For the sixty minutes that followed his arrival, they ordered chest x-rays and ran multiple tests. They fought to stabilise his heart as it fluctuated between being bradycardic (irregularly slow heart rate) to tachycardic (a heart rate over 100 beats per minute) the next. Finally, just after 9:45 pm, he went into cardiac arrest. She went on to say that they had performed CPR for almost 20 minutes. That's where I stopped her abruptly before she could say any more. My body went numb, my heart rate quickened, and my skin felt clammy. I looked her straight in her eyes and asked her calmly, "where's my husband?" She paused and with tears in her eyes... there it was. At the age of 30, Clive Clarence Alexis Harewood, better known as Benny, died at a quarter past ten on Tuesday, April the 14th, 2015.

Many times, I've recalled how I reacted after being told that my husband had just died. I'm gonna be honest with you, I laughed. It was a nervous laugh. The type of sound you make when you think something is a joke and everyone else will laugh with you. In this case, no one else was laughing, and after a split second of uncomfortable silence, the doctor took my hand and led me to where he was. I kept thinking that this was still some sick joke and that at any moment, I would see the funny side of it when I saw him smiling back at me. That moment never came, and when I opened the emergency treatment room door, my heart sank. I stood very still and just stared at him for a minute. I slowly planted one foot in front of the other and walked over to where he lay. Every step was accompanied by an internalised scream that vibrated through every part of my body, pleading with him to get up and move. I finally reached the edge of the hospital bed and scanned his body up and down for some sign of hope that it was not true. But his chest was not rising up and down; the vein that used to pulsate on the left side of his neck was still, and the slight snoring sound he made whilst at rest was silent. My handsome, lifeless husband did not move. He was not sleeping, he was dead. I placed my hand on his face, and he was still warm, which caught me by surprise. I remember I kissed his eyes, laid my head on his chest, and said, "If I didn't tell you I loved you enough, I'm sorry! If I didn't show you that I loved you enough, I'm so sorry!". At the end of the hospital bed, his clothes and other belongings were in a bag on the floor. His red and grey striped jumper. Grey chinos, his wallet, chain, and shoes. Isn't it funny the things that you remember? The room was silent and still when the chaplain brought in a chair for me to sit on. I sat down, staring at him, thinking, what in Jesus 's name am I going to do now? I was alone, thousands of miles away from either of our families and friends. I didn't want to wake anyone up with this type of news. After about ten minutes of stillness, I suddenly remembered something that we had talked about countless times; the body being a vessel that houses the soul, and when the soul leaves, the body's mission is complete. At that moment, I felt an overwhelming presence in the hospital room that I knew was him, saying to me, 'it's time to go, baby. I'm not here, and I need to get you home safe'. How I drove home from the hospital is still a miracle and a blur. I am sure I was in autopilot or survival mode, or both. But I do believe that for the hours that followed Benny's spirit talked and guided me through everything I needed to do step by step.

When the hospital had called earlier that evening, I had left Jacob with our neighbours. I didn't know what was going to greet me when I got there. So, leaving him with them while he slept seemed like and was, in hindsight, the best decision I could have made. They had been such a blessing to us from the moment that we had moved in. Welcoming, caring, showing us the ropes, like our surrogate parents. They were the first people I had to tell that Benny was not going to be coming home. That sound of shock, disbelief, and sadness became an all too familiar sound over the days and weeks ahead. After a shot of whiskey and about 20 minutes of preparing myself to walk back in the home that would never feel the same again, I scooped Jacob up in my arms, walked through our front door and placed him in our bed. Watching him sleep was one of the most painful feelings that I have ever felt. Knowing that his whole world had changed whilst he slept, blissfully unaware of the tragic news I would soon have to tell him.

CHAPTER 2

A DISASTER CALLED DEATH

When I think of some of the various types of
disasters that there are, they generally fit into two
categories, natural and man-made.

Natural	Man-Made
Earthquakes	War
Floods & Landslides	Anthropogenic (man-made) climate change
Hurricanes, Tornados & Cyclones	Acts of Terrorism
Volcanoes	Fires
Wildfires	Hazardous Material Spills

Wikipedia tells us that in short, a natural disaster is a major
adverse event resulting from natural processes of the earth.

Whilst man-made disasters are a result of anthropogenic
hazards caused by human action or inaction. Following the

immediate impact of a natural disaster, emergency response agencies start their processes, rescue and evacuation services are deployed and humanitarian aid is sent to help people. Here is a question that I have asked myself throughout my grief journey. Where does death sit in these categories of disasters and what is the real disaster? Is it the death of the person we love? Is it the painful grief journey that follows? Or is it the fact we will never be the same person after experiencing loss? Speaking from my own experience, I don't think death fits into any category and if I am to be totally honest, I think the real disaster is all three of these things as well as all the mini devastations that hit us along the road of bereavement.

The Immediate Aftermath of Loss

After laying our son Jacob in our bed and watching him sleep, I moved around our home from room to room, inhaling memories. I desperately tried to salvage any sense of what Benny may have done from the time I kissed him goodbye that morning. The undrunk cup of tea I had made him before I left to go to work was by the edge of the sink with some dishes; so, he had eaten that day. I had left him sleeping on the couch, where he had slept for the previous two nights so as not to disturb my sleep; the sheets he used were, as usual, neatly folded up in our bedroom. He had cut his hair, presumably that afternoon, and uncharacteristically left the hair and clippers in the bathroom. I took the dustpan and brush and started to clear it up. As I was sweeping his hair I could smell him, so I quickly bundled it up into a tiny ziplock bag so I would be able to retain the smell of him for as long as I could. Hair can keep the scent of a person for a very long time, so you can imagine how often I pulled open that ziplock bag and visited his scent to try and feel close to him.

After about 30 minutes of unsuccessfully and frantically trying to piece together his last day in our home, I felt an overwhelming sense of calm come over me. At that moment I found a candle, lit it and went to the one place in our home that truly belonged to him … his art table. Drawing had been a safe place for him to escape to and the one thing you could always find that he had with him was a pencil. Many years before, we had visited a tattoo parlour. I had got some musical notes inked on my wrist to signify my love of music and he had decided to put a piece of his own art on his inner forearm. It was a pencil with wings and a little man riding on top of it, with the words 'Free to Sketch' written on the pencil. Many years later I saw that he had the letter 'A' written in the rubber at the end of the pencil; I naively asked him what 'A' meant and he looked at me, smiled that big smile and said 'A' is for 'Alisa'.

In the following hours after lighting the candle I sat on the floor in our front room, where his spirit guided me through every phone call. I felt him hold me in his arms whilst I called his mother in Barbados to tell her that her eldest child and only son was dead. I felt him with me when I had to call my parents in England and try to explain that 'he's gone mum' meant that the son-in-law that she had loved like her own son had died. The endless calls to family, my work, his work and our friends seemed never-ending as the darkness outside my window turned to daylight. A couple of hours earlier I had called a close friend of mine and asked if she would be able to come over. Without hesitation she arrived 20 minutes later and sat with me, in silence for the most part. Just having her there was such a comfort as Jacob awoke and I put on the best performance of my life. "Daddy had to go to work early, son, and mummy is not feeling very well so Aunt Claudia is going to take you to school. Also, I have a big surprise - Auntie Kham is going to collect you from school so you can stay and play with Shomari for a couple of days." I needed to buy myself some time as I had no idea how I was going to get through the days ahead.

Within the next 24 hours shock kicked in and it was time to decide - fight or flight? I did what I always do when my back is up against a wall; I dug deep and - got on with what I had to do. I am a doer. I find solutions to problems; that is what I do best. Flight was not an option! I knew that in the days that followed I would have to go into the deepest parts of myself and uncover hidden depths in order for me to start to arrange his funeral. In the five days that followed I went into full on project manager mode:

- I collected his car from the doctors and went back to the hospital to get more details and his belongings.

- I started the after death & funeral process which was made more complex as I wanted to take his body back to Barbados and bury him there.

- I had to pick out a coffin and his burial clothes on day three so that when his mother & sister arrived, they would not have to see him in the morgue.

- I had to see the sadness and concern for me on my family's face, both those that arrived in the US and the ones back home in the UK over video calls.

- I had to gather the strength to see his mother, sister and aunt as they arrived from Barbados.

- I had to think about finances and budgets for what was going to be a very expensive process and funeral.

However, nothing could have prepared me for the most horrific moment of all; seeing the confusion on Jacob's little face after telling him that he will never be able to see his daddy again... I have no words for this.

The Response Team

Many of the people that were first on the scene were friends that I had known for less than a year or so. They would prove to be invaluable to me in those first few days. They became my family until my family was able to arrive from other parts of the world. Many of them selflessly gave up their time, resources, homes, money and so many other things to come to mine and Jacob's aid. We had food parcels delivered daily, collections and donations made. My workplace paid for some of my family to get to me within 24 hours of Benny's death and organisational plans were changed to accommodate some senior leaders' rerouting travel plans to come and make sure we were ok. I am unsure how I would have survived without them and thank you is too small a phrase to express my gratitude for the love that they showed us.

During the immediate aftermath of Benny's death, I was naturally oblivious to anything that was going on outside of my peripheral vision. I got up every day and was focused on just getting through the day, getting things done and getting him back to his paternal family in Barbados, so that we could lay his body to rest. If I am being brutally honest, outside of what I was going through I really didn't spend any time factoring in other people's pain. Well, that's a lie, I did worry about Benny's mum, dad and sisters and obviously I worried about Jacob. I called us our 'grief bubble'. My feelings during this time and for many years after was that if you were anyone outside of my grief bubble you could not relate or empathise with what we were all going through. In preparation for writing this book I spent time interviewing members of my family. It is indescribable, the process and experience of spending time, five years later, asking my family questions like:

- Where were you when I called to tell you that Benny had died?

- What happened within the family in the 24 - 48 hours that followed his death?

- How did you feel during your time in Barbados for the funeral?

- How have you coped with your own grief since his death?

- What two pieces of advice would you give to family members of those that are helping a loved one deal with grief?

- How would you describe the journey that you have seen me go through since Benny's death?

I was filled with anxiety and fear! Would anyone be prepared to talk to me about how they felt? How would it affect them and how would I react to the things that they might say? Would it destroy my progress or worse, bring up deep rooted blockages? There were so many reasons to not know but they were outweighed by more reasons to ask. I really felt that it would benefit both them and me. I was not wrong. My family were actually carrying the sadness of my loss and seeing the pain I was going through; they carried their own personal grief but hid it in the shadows and some of them still have not grieved properly as they had to suppress it to help me. Some people knew I was screaming for help at key times in my grief journey but did not know how to help or what to do for the best. There is a tremendous amount of guilt for those that do not feel that they gave the right amount of support, and some family tensions are still being mended. What I also found out was how huge a positive impact Benny had made within our family. After we moved to the US he kept in touch with my family - possibly more often than I did. During my interviews I was shocked at how many of them said that they had either spoken with, or he had messaged them on a regular basis. One of the many great qualities about him was his ability to listen and show love towards all people, but especially to family.

From the conversations I've had with my nearest and dearest, I would offer these pieces of advice: Try to be honest with your family and friends at various intervals of your journey. Don't get me wrong, they do not need to be your priority; your healing should be your primary focus. However, letting them know how you feel - the good, the bad and the ugly truth - is better than sitting in silence. Also, circle back at the times you feel strong enough or during the seasons where things are feeling more hopeful and check on how they are doing. You are the one that has felt the immediate impact of the loss but those that love you will be seeing you in pain and may feel paralysed to help, so tell them what you need and how they can help. This leaves less room for the door of ambiguity to be left open. Not saying anything at all can cause long term damage and turn into one of those additional mini devastations I spoke about earlier. We are all human beings who have feelings and hurt, so ask for forgiveness in advance for the things that may cause subconscious offence. It is okay to be vulnerable and show you're hurting as it opens a pathway for others to show you, they care, but also know they can show their pain too.

The Last Goodbye

Even though Benny did not tell me what type of funeral he would want, one thing I was certain of was that he would have wanted to be buried back home in his beloved

Barbados. When I spoke to his mum about cremating him or burying him, we decided that we had to take his body back in one piece and not in ashes. His family and friends needed their time with him and I 100% understood. Even though this would mean that Jacob and I would not be able to visit his burial place on a regular basis, in my heart I knew that I would have Jacob, his living legacy with me, so it was only fair that I laid him to rest near his family. Getting his body back to Barbados would prove to be a waiting game as I was determined to travel back with him. I did not want him to travel alone. In my own way I wanted to keep hold of him for as long as I could. Some would say I was being selfish, and maybe I was but all I knew was that I needed to hold his hand until it was no longer an option; until he had to go into the ground and until I had no choice but to say my last goodbye. Finally, a week and a half later, on Thursday the 23rd of April, while my sister Machalea and I were at home getting ready to start our day, I got the call from the funeral home: 'We have been able to get you all out on a flight that leaves today!'. I can remember feeling relief and anxiety all at the same time, as I was one step closer to getting him home but also one step closer to letting him go. My sister and I rushed around with Jacob getting last minute things done as we had about 4 hours to get ready and get to Detroit Metropolitan Wayne County Airport. I had travelled in and out of the international terminal so many times over the previous three years for business that I could time my route there like clockwork. What I was not prepared for was the domestic terminal operating under a completely different process, having a child with me, having my sister with me, flying at peak travel time and just the stress of making sure we did not miss the flight, which was being routed via Miami.

After the most stressful arrival and check-in in my life we were all finally sat on the aeroplane. I remember feeling this sense of peace knowing that Benny's body was on the flight with us. He had been in the funeral home all this time, so I was glad to know that we were reunited as a family. When we arrived in Miami all I could concern myself with was making sure that his body had arrived safely. We made our way to the baggage area to collect our luggage. My state of mind had me thinking that a packaged-up surfboard was him; I remember my sister calmly having to explain to me that he would not be coming out of baggage claim and that his body would have been taken somewhere secure. With that in mind and with my anxiety levels at an all-time high as our luggage had not arrived from Detroit, I went to the information desk to ask if I could get confirmation that his body had arrived safely. What I was greeted with upon arrival at the desk was what I can only describe as the lowest level of sympathy and biggest lack of empathy I have ever experienced in my life. I was abruptly told by a pair of Customer Service Representatives - a term I use very loosely - that they couldn't give me any information. Even when I explained, with tears in my eyes, what had occurred over the previous ten days, I was met with a barrage of armed security guards. The representatives at the desk had called them as they felt that, due to my anger at their lack of empathy, I was a big enough threat to warrant being escorted away, in front of my 4-year-old son (who was being comforted by my sister), to a side room. Luckily Jesus had my back covered as in that side room I was questioned by a lady who asked me to explain my side of what had occurred. As I sobbed my eyes out trying to explain my situation and that I just wanted to find out if my husband had arrived safely at their airport, she comforted me and kindly told me that they could not give out that information due to protocol. After about 10 minutes of me calming down and the security guards apologising to me for having to be called out in the first place, she was able to let me know that 'a body' had arrived at the airport from my flight. I was so grateful for her reassurance. It was the first time that I had actually let any pain out of my body since his death. Sure, it was not the best of timing, but I had suddenly, for the first time, started to feel this uncontrollable wave of sadness and it could not be contained. I was escorting my beloved Benny home to be buried. Ninety minutes later I was reunited with my sister and Jacob. I could see the relief on her poor face. She had been by my side since she had arrived in the US. I had always been the strong older sister, so to see me break down in such a public way in the middle of an airport must have rocked her. After a cuddle and reassuring her that I was okay we made our way to the hotel that we were staying at overnight before our final flight back to Barbados the following morning. By the time we arrived there we were all exhausted. Luckily, we had packed overnight clothes in our hand luggage and were able to wash away the misery of what had been such a traumatic day. I put Jacob to sleep and watched my sister doze off, the stillness of our hotel room was filled with a fog of pain. I had nowhere to run to and I felt this overwhelming weight of sorrow that made me want to scream as loud as I could for as long as I could. Instead, I put pen to paper and wrote the first journal entry in my diary.

April 24th, 2015 - 12:13am

'My pain & sorrow is currently at a dark moment, everywhere I turn you are there but absent. My faith has been crippled by grief & me can't feel the Lord holding my heart together. I have been unable to talk about the wonder of you today so feel distant, like you are not with me but elsewhere.

Why have you left me! You promised that you would stay! I feel angry and cheated today. Memories that were so helpful for me to recall are now, in this moment bringing me an unbearable emptiness. My anguish and pain I know is the devil & I want him to go from around me but I feel so much pain. My tears are like a faucet and if I start crying I am afraid I won't be able to stop.

Please help me move through this moment, Lord!'

After a day and a half, I finally got Benny's body back to his beloved Barbados. Arriving back to a place that was filled with so many memories felt like walking around a haunted house. Every place I went to was filled with his smile, his laugh, his scent. Constant flashbacks of moments we had shared during our seven-year love affair.

I honestly can't give you any details of the days that followed my arrival into Barbados as it was a haze of seeing more and more grief in the eyes of his family and friends. Then there was the arrival of my parents into Barbados for the funeral, the look of sadness at the loss of a man they called their son and the pain of not being able to take away my pain ever visible on their faces. On top of this I had all the fine-tuning of arrangements to consider, alongside my internal self-preparation for the funeral. The three weeks that had flown by had left me physically, mentally, and emotionally exhausted. But I still had one last thing to do - the speech.

I'm sure that you can relate to the fact that trying to write a eulogy, a speech, or a few words to read out aloud is one of the most challenging moments of one's life. Mainly because all you want to do is say all the things you never got a chance to say, to the one person who's not there to listen. I felt like I needed to maintain a fine balance of showing a robust exterior while exuding enough but not too much emotion, so as not to make others feel uncomfortable. In other words, show enough of my pain so that people will see how much I loved and missed him, but toned down so that it was respectful and dignified.

I have always found the West Indian funeral traditions a bit over the top. Open coffins; lots of traditional hymns; the multitudes of people that come to say goodbye. And all the flowers at the graveside, covering the final resting place. Yet there I was, having to live it in high definition. He never told me what he wanted; he always changed the subject whenever I asked and said, ' You'll know.'

I believed he would have liked to have been cremated, with his ashes scattered in the ocean and one big jam down (a big Caribbean party) on the beach. Yet I gave his paternal family the service they needed. Not because anyone forced me to. The simple fact is he would have done the same thing if I had gone first, and he'd not known what I wanted. Also, if I am being honest, I felt a considerable amount of guilt. He had left that beautiful island of Barbados - the country that he adored - and the family and friends he loved with all his heart and followed me, and I felt like I had not taken care of him. I brought him back to them in a box, so the very least I could do was allow them to mourn him in 'their' way.

In the end, I wrote my speech the night before his funeral. Remembering the man, he was, I focused more on the message I felt he would want me to give to those he had left behind. The funeral filled me with an indescribable emptiness; it felt like we were arranging a special event where we knew the guest of honour would never arrive. I don't have anything else to say about a moment in time that was both about celebrating my husband's life and mourning his death—what a parallel calamity.

What I do want to do is share with you the speech that I wrote and read out at his funeral. It is not only to give you an idea of the type of man he was but also to inspire you as you read this book. The pain of your loss may be recent, or it may have been some time ago. Regardless of when it was, my deepest desire is that this book will give you hope! The hope and belief that one day you will be able to love life and live it again.

The Speech

There are many milestone dates in our life that hold different types of significance to us all. The date we are born into this world, the date we may commit our life to Jesus. The date some of us get married, have our first child, and ultimately the date that we pass over into the next life.

One of the most significant dates in my life was on Tuesday, March the 11th 2008. The day that I met a man that was to become my friend first, boyfriend, fiancé, father of our son. And then, on another significant date, January the 8th, 2011, my husband and best friend. He was and still is my inspiration, and I am so very proud to be standing here as his wife. We came from two very separate worlds, and on paper, no one thought it would last. We became the dream team against all the odds, with our son Jacob being our biggest achievement.

I had 7 years of memories that will sustain my heart for an eternity. And as a father, he did more in 4 and a half years with our son than most fathers do in a lifetime. Husband and friend, thank you for making me better. Thank you for the gift of motherhood and thank you for showing me what true love really is.

I don't need to spend the rest of my time telling you the type of man my husband was. As you are all very aware of the many attributes he possessed. That beautiful contagious smile. His addictive positivity for life and love. And the supernatural artistic creativity that oozed from every fibre of his being. What he would want is for me to give you a message from him. And the message has the most simplistic of meanings. Love one another and live your life by inspiring others to be better.

I have a poem that I want to read to you by an unknown author. It was sent to me via email from my friend the day after my husband passed away. It is a poem that I believe he would want me to share with you all. In the hope that even through the pain and sorrow that we all feel in this moment. We can take time to celebrate the wonderful life he was living. And that it gives you some comfort through this very painful and dark storm.'

Don't grieve for me; for now, I'm free,
I'm following the path Jesus laid for me.
I took his hand when I heard his call,
I turned my back and left it all.

I could not stay another day,
To laugh, to love, to work, to play.
Tasks left undone must stay that way,
I've found that peace at the close of the day
If my parting has left a void,
Then fill it with remembered joy.

A friendship shared, a laugh, a kiss,
Ah, yes, these things I too will miss.

Be not burdened with times of sorrow,
I wish you the sunshine of tomorrow.

My life's been full, I savoured much,
Good friends, good times, a loved one's touch,
Perhaps my time seemed all too brief,
Don't lengthen it now with undue grief.
Lift up your heart and share with me,
Jesus wanted me now. He set me free.

CHAPTER 3

FUNCTIONAL GRIEF

I would like to take a little pause right now from my journey and experiences to introduce you to what the physiological & psychological response to loss is. Knowing how your body and mind function through grief is really important. You might be thinking, why is it important? Why should I even care about how it responds? Well, the simple truth is that there is actually a process to grieving. Don't confuse what I am saying here. Every person's psychological grief journey is unique to them but the stages of grief and the way in which our bodies react are identical. With this in mind, as you read through this chapter, I want you to remember a couple of key points:

1. We all go through the identical physiological responses to loss.

2. The stages of grief are the same but will be journeyed differently by every individual.

3. The differentiator is how we psychologically choose to function through our personal grief journey.

G.A.S.

The impact of emotional shock is also known as emotional or psychological trauma. After the extraordinarily stressful loss of someone that we love, both our physical and mental state is threatened and as a result our fight or flight switch is triggered. The fight or flight response, also known as acute stress response, is activated when certain hormones are released into our body, preparing it to either stay and deal with a threat (fight) or run away to safety (flight). This response is also the first of three stages of what is known as the General Adaptation Syndrome (G.A.S) - a process identified by a medical doctor and researcher called Hans Selye in the 1920's that describes the physiological changes the body goes through when under stress.

When we first experience the immediate impact of loss we have what G.A.S. describes as the 'Alarm' reaction, which consists of the initial symptoms the body experiences when under stress. Your heart rate increases, your adrenal gland releases cortisol (a stress hormone), and you receive a boost of adrenaline, which increases energy. I remember feeling this immediately and over the following days after Benny died.

The next stage is called the 'Resistance' stage. After your fight or flight response, you start to adapt and process the immediate trauma that has occurred; your body starts to repair itself by releasing a lower level of cortisol whilst your heart rate and blood pressure start to normalise. However, when we lose someone the structured pattern that our brain ordinarily works in is seismically disturbed. If we are unable to come to terms with the trauma that has happened our brain struggles to return to its original structured pattern which means, we will continue to have trouble making sense of anything around us. We go into a place of denial; we lose the ability to concentrate, can become irrational, irritable or both. The continued stress this puts on our bodies is immense. Because of this the body stays on high alert in an attempt to cope and, as we are not built to handle this level of stress indefinitely, ultimately, we start to move into the third stage of G.A.S which is 'Exhaustion'. This final stage is the result of a prolonged period of chronic stress. I know this stage very well as I subconsciously stayed in the 'resistance' stage for an extremely long time. I filled my time and my deep feeling of mourning with many things that I felt would absorb the shock of not having 'my person' alive. Having to continue my life without him led me down a spiral of dependency to sex, alcohol and marijuana and, after two years of resistance, I was exhausted both mentally and physically, which caused the implosion leading to my mental breakdown.

Five Stages of Grief Theory

Let me take a moment to explain the theory developed by psychiatrist Elisabeth Kübler-Ross. Her theory suggests that we go through five distinct stages of grief after the loss of a loved one:

Denial
Anger

Bargaining
Depression
And finally, Acceptance.

Having read so many books about the grief cycle, I naively
thought that I would transition from one stage to another
with ease—what a joke. The reality is that these stages do
100% exist. I also believe that they exist in the order that they
are outlined, with one caveat. The most essential thing to
remember is that there is no neat, orderly transition from one
step to the next. It's more like you move from one stage into
another, back to another, then on to the next one. You can
stay in one stage for a hot second then, without warning,
move to another and stay there for what can seem like an
eternity. If I could give you one piece of advice, it is this:
There is no exact science to how you move through the
stages of grief. It's individual to you, it's unique, and
ultimately, it's how you choose to function through them that
matters. In my experience you cannot try to cheat them or
skip a step. In fact, that is counterproductive as you will
almost certainly find yourself going back to that stage and will
have to overcome it at some point. There is no other way
than to confront your feelings and talk them through.
Healing will, and does take time, so be kind to yourself and
note that one thing it cannot be, as much as we would like, is
rushed.

Complicated Grief

My grief turned into what they call 'Complicated Grief'. I have struggled long and hard with this definition as I am unsure if there is such a thing as 'Simple Grief'. Grief is grief, right?! However, they do say that prolonged grief - that which lasts more than one year - can turn into grief that ends up dominating your life. So, I have come to terms with the fact that, if this is what the definition means, then I am guilty as charged. Symptoms of prolonged grief may include:

- Intense sadness and emotional pain.
- Feelings of emptiness and hopelessness.
- Yearning to be reunited with the deceased.
- Preoccupation with the deceased or with the circumstances of the death.
- Difficulty engaging in happy memories of the lost person.
- Avoidance of reminders of the deceased.
- A reduced sense of identity.
- Detachment and isolation from surviving friends and family.
- Lack of desire to pursue personal interests or plans.

I was in a continuous state of mourning for many, many years and to make matters worse I kept this fact secret. When others were looking, I acted as though I was fine but when I was alone, I would revert to my grief. Some days it became so tiresome playing the part of a survivor that I could not wait to get home, put Jacob to bed, turn off all the lights, pull the covers over my head and wallow in loneliness. Weekends were my favourite time as I could lock everything out. Suffice to say that the person who saw this side of me was my son, who must have been so alone himself as I would park him in front of the television all weekend, only coming out of my room to feed him. The immediate impact of my isolation was not evident until many years later, when I was in a better place to help him move through the delayed impact of loss. Having seen how counselling had changed me, he knew that it might help him so, at the age of 10 years old and five years after his father's death, he went through a season of bereavement counselling. Which brings me onto the importance of counselling.

The Importance of Counselling

Everyone grieves in their own way and no one journey will be the same. Some people may feel better after six months or a year. It took me four years to journey to the acceptance stage of grief. I suppressed my grief and refused to accept that there was a process that could help me survive the resistance stage of G.A.S. and journey through the stages of grief in a healthy way.

Psychologist J. W. Worden created a model for coping with the death of a loved one. He divided the bereavement process into four tasks:

1. To accept the reality of the loss.
2. To work through the pain of grief.
3. To adjust to life without your loved one.
4. To maintain a connection to the person that has died while moving on with life.

I could not accept any of these and in most cases found unhealthy comfort blankets to hide under for as long as I could. A piece of advice that without fail you MUST listen to; is this: Functioning through grief can only happen if you focus on the tasks of mourning by speaking to someone that is a trained counsellor or therapist. Here are my top tips for finding the right person for you to speak to based on my experience:

1. Find someone that specialises in grief/bereavement counselling as they will know the process that needs to happen in order for you to travel through the painful stages of grief. Ask someone you trust for a recommendation. On both occasions I found mine and my son's counsellor through asking people I trusted.

2. Tell your family and friends that you are going to be seeing a counsellor / therapist. There is no shame in it and it will also help them to understand what you are going through.

3. Speak to your GP or ask at your work for referral plans that are available to you.

4. Decide on a budget. I had to make sure I prioritised this as therapists can be expensive. There are however a number of options - funded charities, free online resources and also speaking to the therapist about the budget you can afford. They may be able to work out a payment plan for you or even refer you to someone that is in your price range.

5. Go the distance and don't give up. There will be times when you will have to deal with some very heavy stuff, but you have to travel through the grief to get to the glory.

I wish I had understood the importance of this earlier on. Would it have changed my journey? I absolutely believe it would have. Would I be writing this book? Probably not, as my journey would not have revealed to me the impact that my relationship with Jesus has had on transforming my life. I cannot stress to you enough that, even with my strong faith, seeking help from a professional was the key to unlocking the pain, healing and learning how to repair my life.

CHAPTER 4

DEAR DIARY...

During the early months I found that I was just trying to get myself through the day and trying to be a good mother was all I could focus on and deal with. My writing was a safe place, where no judgement on me was made. It was a place where I could write out my truth. I have found that journaling, writing blogs, poetry and ultimately writing this book has and continues to be an outlet to offload my private pain. I started to write my thoughts and feelings down from around day four after Benny's death. It started off with me telling my journal all the things I wanted to tell him about day-to-day stuff. In some strange way it made me feel closer to him. After only a few short days my words became an outlet for my pain, and I have been writing in some form or another ever since.

Many of you may be feeling like you have so much to say but are unable to because of the pain that you're in. Let me share with you some of my journal entries so that you understand that I know where you are and what you are going through. I felt a myriad of different feelings and emotions that overloaded and overwhelmed me. It was like I had a long piece of rope tied around my ankles and attached at the other end of that rope was an anchor that would consistently pull me down into the water. Some days my head would feel like it was above water because the tide was low and some days it would feel like the high tide was submerging me. I would feel weighed down, begging for someone or something to cut the rope so that I could be free to breathe again. Finding an outlet - a source of release - for all the emotions that came during this season became essential; emotions as painful as this *cannot* stay inside forever... Trust me, if you internalise all the pain that you are feeling it will have nowhere to go. When pain has nowhere to go it gets stored down like a pressure cooker waiting to explode. In order to release the pressure and the pain we might seek pleasure in ways that can be destructive and only give us temporary relief. The pleasure you get from releasing the pressure in an unhealthy way can then lead to guilt and shame that drives a cycle of dependency and addiction. This can become a slippery slope, leading to the destruction of your life and those that you love.

The cycle of dependency refers to how people can develop unhealthy habits or behaviours to cope with their grief. Here's a simplified breakdown:

1. Trigger or loss: Something happens that causes a person to experience deep grief, like the death of a loved one or a major life change.

2. Coping mechanism: To deal with the intense emotions and pain of grief, people may turn to things like drugs, alcohol, or other addictive behaviours to feel better temporarily.

3. Temporary relief: The coping mechanism provides a brief sense of relief from the grief, offering a temporary escape from the intense emotions.

4. Negative consequences: Relying on unhealthy coping mechanisms can lead to negative effects, like damage to relationships, health problems, and neglecting important responsibilities.

5. Guilt and shame: As the negative consequences pile up, people may feel guilty or ashamed about their dependency, realising that it's not helping them heal from their grief.

6. Increased dependency: To avoid the guilt, shame, and pain of grief, some individuals may increase their reliance on the unhealthy coping mechanisms, creating a cycle that's harder to break.

7. Worsening consequences: As the dependency grows, the negative consequences can become even worse, making it harder for the person to heal and move forward from their grief.

8. Awareness and desire for change: Eventually, people may recognise that their dependency isn't helping them and they want to make positive changes to cope with their grief more effectively.

9. Healing and support: Seeking help from professionals or support groups and finding healthier ways to cope with grief is crucial for breaking the cycle of dependency and promoting healing.

10. Relapse: Sometimes, people may temporarily go back to their old coping mechanisms or unhealthy behaviours. Relapses are normal and can be seen as opportunities for growth and learning.

Understanding the cycle of dependency in grief will help you realise the challenges they you may face or be facing and the importance of seeking support and healthy coping strategies or as like to call them healthy comfort blankets during your grieving process.

Throughout my journey I battled with this cycle of dependency in multiple stages, which I will talk about in many of the following chapters. The one thing that brought me out of every corrosive dependency cycle was my relationship with Jesus and knowing that he loves me despite how I chose to deal with my pain. He continues to make me realise that his love for me is unconditional even during this season. In order to step into a place of healing I had to stop masking and trying to numb my sadness because it was leading me down a narrow one-way street of destruction. He reminded me that my gift for writing was a way for me to get my hurt out until I was strong enough to start to talk it out. So that is what I did. I bought a notebook and every time it was high tide and I felt submerged, I wrote. Sometimes a lot and sometimes a little; sometimes every day and sometimes once a week. But it was a lifeline for me as storing inside all the things I was feeling and experiencing would have been so damaging. Ironically, the times I stopped writing were the times that I tried to numb my pain with toxic outlets, which felt good for very short periods of time. Writing may not be your outlet of choice but if you feel ready how about recording a video diary or creating some art, (painting or creating a collage). It can be any outlet that you choose but I want to challenge yourself to start letting your feelings out.

I want to share with you some of the diary excerpts that I wrote during the first couple of months after Benny passed away. I have kept all the excerpts completely unedited from my original diary entries as I want you to understand that I know first-hand that the grief you are dealing with may sound like confused noise, but it is such a normal and necessary part of the journey.

My Diary Excerpts

2nd May 2015 - 3:10 pm

Well today is the day that I am leaving Barbados to go and spend a week in the UK and I have emotions that I can't explain. Happiness that I brought you your body home; sadness as I miss you and I wish none of this was happening. So much love for and from the family, both yours and mine. Hope that in time the pain will dull bit by bit and memories will fill my heart with joy instead of sorrow. I still think that I am in a state of shock. I feel you telling me to 'let go' but another part wants to hold on in the hope that you will be at home back in the USA when we get back there. Moment by moment step by step Jesus first, family second and everything else last. The Clive Harewood chapter of my life has been filled with a million emotions with the biggest achievement of it all being Jacob Zion Harewood our son. I will try and be the best mum and dad that I can, and I know that you will guide us with safety, love and the pride you always showed. I wasn't perfect, I know, but I am truly grateful for all you have taught and showed me. You truly made me better and stronger, and I will always have you as the lion within me. See you later alligator Mr Clive Clarence Alexis Harewood, my Benny, my friend my love. I fly away from Barbados with Jesus who will guide me to my new purpose. I will do as you always asked of me when you were alive. I will try and take it slow; I will try not to work, work, work and I will try and live my life to the fullest. I wish it was with you, but you fly now and be free; spread peace, love and kindness throughout the world as an Angel and remember to come and see me in my dreams from time-to-time love always your wife, Axxx

5th May 2015 - 9:55 am

Well today neither feels like a good day or a bad day. I want to be true to my emotions today and feel the pain of loss. I don't want it to overtake me but I do want to 'FEEL' today. The loss of you hits me in my face sometimes like a train...SMACK!! When I realise that you never get over grief, all seems so hopeless, and I start to feel weak and alone. I call on the Lord as my refuge and strength, but I need to pray harder as it doesn't dull the pain. I need to get to Jacob quickly as I feel detached from you and I need my son, our son's presence around me.

7th May 2015 - 7:51 am

23 days have passed, it seems like longer. Why, why, why????
I feel like I didn't appreciate the man that you were. I feel like I complained internally and externally about all you didn't do and that's why you've been taken away from me. Your

kindness, love and caring nature became lost to me in a world where I had become blinded by the distraction of the everyday. Is this my punishment or is this my purpose? To question everything is human and to believe that there is hope must be centred in faith, but the lines are blurred right now. I am trying to deal with the fact that we have to go home to the USA tomorrow, but I can't help feeling nervous about it all. How will I feel, how will Jacob feel, it all becomes even more real and the hard winding road to healing and recovery begins. I'm just not ready. I still can't believe you're really gone. I know it's happened but when I get home, I really think the enormity of it all will smack me in the face! I will continue to ask Jesus to give me strength and I know that you will continue to give me a safe harbour. I feel you so near sometimes, your energy and your warmth comfort me. I'm going to read my Bible and get the message for the day, love you.

8th May 2015 - 2:30 pm

Well, the day has come for us to return to, what some would call the scene of the crime. We are heading back to the US. I am trying to focus on it being the start of a new life, but I feel like I am trying to convince myself that all is going to be ok. The reality is for the first time in my life I have no idea what 'OK' is supposed to look like. I feel tired!!!

11th May 2015 - 7:00 am

Well today is another first. Taking Jacob to school; going shopping the first time as a twosome and not a threesome. My heart and body hurts today. I miss your presence; I sense that it's far from me and I can hear you talking to me in my mind less and less. The silence is making me feel the enormity and realness of loneliness. I am going to get into my bible today. I think it's time to take off your chain today, I have had it on since the night you died as you left it on the dressing table. I am going to replace it with a memory gift that I will buy with some of the money that you left us... yes, I like that idea.

8:00am - At breakfast Jacob & I were talking about Jesus and the fact that Jacob says he is your boss now. Jacob told me that 'daddy comes to me while I am sleeping' and he hugged himself as he said it. He also told me that Jesus loves me. I asked him why he told me that and he said Jesus told him. I asked him if he could tell me what Jesus looked like and he told me 'Enough now' as he didn't want to talk anymore. Jacob is blessed!

14th May 2015 - 7:35 am

So, it's officially one month since you died! I am now in a phase where I think I am in shock and disbelief that you have really gone. I know that you would not have left us without a fight, but I also know that I should have done more to fight for you. What if I spent that hour before you died thinking positive thoughts about our love instead of trying to find fault about why you had not come home yet? What if I told you to go straight to the ER and took you there on Monday? What if I made you go for a check-up early enough? The what if's go on and on. The void you have left in my soul is unbearable now that reality has kicked in... I MISS U...PLEASE COME BACK!!

15th May 2015 - 8:53 am

Well, I had a good night's sleep considering how much I drank last night. How sad to drink alone with only sadness and pain as company. This morning I need to call on the strength that Jesus has given me, along with the lioness that I know I am to find a way to move forward. My son's happiness and stability is essential. I need to find a way for him to say goodbye. I made the decision not to take him to the funeral, one day you were here and then you were gone. You didn't say goodbye and I am angry at you because of that, so I can only imagine the confusion he feels; poor little boy. I don't feel you around me as I did before but I hope you are with him ALWAYS!!! I need to pray my way through the anger that I feel as I am so mad that Jacob has to go through this and that you didn't take better care of your fucking self. 'I'll beat this asthma' you said. really, really! No you didn't, now we are suffering for your selfish need to beat a disability that you should have taken more bloody seriously...I HATE YOU FOR THIS!!!

20th May 2015 - 5:25 am

The home feels so different without your presence. Empty and lonely! I try to fill it with memories of us but sometimes it's too hard. I am going to have to push myself today. After going back to work a couple of days ago I have one meeting and then I will hide myself in my office and just do emails today. Missing you is so painful baby! I love you.

CHAPTER 5

THE EMPTY SEASON

A New Normal

I was now in a season of sheer emptiness that is so hard to articulate to anyone that has not been through the first three to six months after loss. I believed that trying to get back to some type of routine would be good for me to accelerate my way through grief and in an attempt to normalise my life I made the decision to return to work four weeks after Benny's death. At the beginning of 2015 (the year Benny died), I received a promotion. My hard work had paid off, and I became the first female and black person to become Vice President of a sales and delivery function in the company's twenty-five-year history. I was managing a $30 million business unit, leading a global team spanning three continents. I was the only woman on the North American leadership team and, to top it off, earned the same six-figure salary as my male counterparts. Not bad for a girl that grew up on a council estate and didn't finish university. I had spent the best part of my career working my arse off to become a leader within a global organisation. And here I was, the Vice

President for the North American Managed Services Division.

In late May of 2015, I sat in my first quarterly sales meeting. I had always relished the adrenaline rush that came with the challenge of performance reviews. I prided myself and was known for being in the details, always overachieving and having a plan for every plan. However, this battle was bloody and brutal. I was being quizzed & scrutinised on the lack of revenue, the lack of pipeline growth, and as a result, the negative impact on the overall territories financials. I remember fixing my gaze at the CEO, who was firing the killer bullet questions. This man had been my mentor for the past two years. He knew my capabilities, my strengths and my weaknesses, but yet here he was, firing on all cylinders. All I wanted to do was scream and shout at the top of my lungs… "my husband died; that's why the numbers are not where they need to be! My husband is dead; that's why your revenue target hasn't been hit! My husband is dead; that's why my team has had no direction. I haven't been sunning my bloody self in San Tropez, you arsehole!" But I couldn't say any of those things. I actually did what he had taught me to do during my time working side by side with him. Stay calm, make no excuses, bring only solutions, and never show your weakness as those around you will be able to use it against you. So, I calmly and very unemotionally expressed that I would look at the numbers, we would revise our plan, and we would commit to making up the shortfall in the next quarter. I was a walking, talking contradiction, as none of those things mattered to me anymore, but I knew that I had to be seen to be a leader even amidst my tragedy. The most significant revelation came to me during that meeting. I'd worked all of my career to get to this place, yet at that moment, I wanted to be anywhere else but in that boardroom. The job I had ploughed all of myself into meant nothing without my husband alive to cheer me on. I internally accepted that my career would not satisfy the desire I craved to normalise my life. In fact, it was the very opposite, as in the months ahead, I realised that being a leader in a corporate setting held little to no value for me other than a pay cheque and a materialistic lifestyle that was not going to feed my soul any longer. That meeting ended my love affair with the corporate world, and I was left petrified at what could possibly fill the void that the loss of my husband and now the loss of my career had left.

The Need for Intimacy

This chapter has been the hardest chapter for me to write as there are things that I did during this season that are very taboo and difficult to discuss, especially as I am now a Christian. I contemplated not sharing them at all but realised that if I was not completely authentic and transparent in writing this book then how could I truly look anyone in the face and say that this was all of my truth? So, here goes. After losing the one person in the world that had ever truly understood me, accepted all my flaws, propelled me forward to fulfil my dreams and understood what made me tick. Coupled with the contempt I felt for the career that had given myself and my family great opportunities; but had consumed large quantities of time during our lives together. I had such a profound sense of apathy. Feeling nothing other than the inner turmoil of deep mourning and loss for copious areas of my life led me to need the touch of another man. I could tell you that wanting to be physically intimate with a man made me feel more secure and filled a chasm of loneliness. I could tell you that there is scientific evidence proving that having sex releases feel-good neurotransmitters and pain-reducing hormones that can help to relieve you from the pain of grief temporarily. Whilst these points are accurate, the fact of the matter is I just wanted to feel loved. I missed Benny with every fibre of my being. I didn't want a replacement for him or even really care about the two guys I had sex with on a regular basis during those first six to twelve months. What I needed was to just 'feel'. I felt pain, I felt numb, I felt disappointment at the cruel curveball that life had thrown me, and I needed desperately to balance those feelings out with love and intimacy.

Many years later, I uncovered and untangled through my counselling process some deeply rooted affliction attached to a sexual trauma I experienced just before I turned 20. I had then subconsciously spent the following 20 years of my life equating love and sex as going hand in hand. So, at this stage in my grief journey, when the only feeling I thought would balance out the pain was love, and, as love automatically equalled sex in my mind, that's what I craved.

In the previous chapter I introduced you to the 'Cycle of Dependency'. Well sex became my first unhealthy comfort blanket and a dependency crutch which gave me temporary relief. This support bandage always left me with feelings of regret and shame, which would propel me right back to my pain. It was a vicious cycle of dependency, so much so that the guilt and shame I internalised didn't even make it to the pages of my journal. It festered in me, holding hands with the resistance and denial of my grief, leading me to make wholly irrational and questionable decisions like introducing an old love affair back into my life and, therefore, into Jacob's. You can imagine the confusion that this must have had on a 4-year-old boy! He lost his daddy, and now I bring this man into his life only to have him leave again many months later. I have spent an enormous amount of time beating myself up about that, but I have had to learn to forgive myself for past mistakes; otherwise, I would get ensnared in the morass of regret, which is not a healthy place for healing to grow.

I would love to tell you that I only visited this detrimental comfort blanket during the early stages of my grief, but I would be lying. It would take me almost four years and a lot of counselling to unpick the reason sex had become the driving force in many past relationships and the place I would run to, to feel loved. It would take me four years to understand that the only love that I needed was the love of Jesus who has repaired so many parts of me, allowing me to be free and live a hope filled life with a promised future of finding a new sense of self-worth and value in loving and seeing myself as he does.

He Carried Me

Looking back on the first six to nine months I can tell you honestly that even though I was praying to Jesus for help and support I did not feel it was helping me get through day by day. I was lovesick and the cure was sex and intimacy from a man to help me feel loved. I had to reconcile that the identity I had found in my career no longer satisfied or sustained me. And being a single parent engulfed me with feelings of fear and bitterness. I had not signed up for any of this. So much of these months were me trying to feel anything other than profound loss. I was trying to move out of the 'Resistance Stage' of G.A.S; however, I was still in denial that he was dead and the domino effect this had started as it knocked down so many other areas of loss as a result. I kept praying and keeping Jesus close, but at times I lost hope that He was with me. How could he be if I was feeling all of this? However, he was there. There is a very famous poem that beautifully illustrates what Jesus did for me during this period of profound sadness; the poem is called Footprints. The poem is a metaphor about faith, resilience, and the presence of a higher power during times of struggle.

One night I dreamed a dream.
As I was walking along the beach with my Lord.
Across the dark sky flashed scenes from my life.
For each scene, I noticed two sets of footprints in the sand,
One belonging to me and one to my Lord.

After the last scene of my life flashed before me,
I looked back at the footprints in the sand.
I noticed that at many times along the path of my life,
especially at the very lowest and saddest times,
There was only one set of footprints.

This really troubled me, so I asked the Lord about it.
"Lord, you said once I decided to follow you,

You'd walk with me all the way.
But I noticed that during the saddest and most troublesome
times of my life,
There was only one set of footprints.
I don't understand why, when I needed You the most,
You would leave me."

He whispered, "My precious child,
I love you and will never leave you,
Never, ever, during your trials and testing's,
When you saw only one set of footprints,
It was then that I carried you."

This period of my life was, by all accounts, the start of my healing. I can look back on it now and say that, but at the time, it was me just trying to survive life after the immediate loss. What I do know is this; I was walking, I was breathing, I was eating, and I was sleeping. But it was Jesus who was carrying me through it all because, during that time, I could not do it by myself.

CHAPTER 6

THE ANGRY SEASON

Barbados

I had decided not to make any significant decisions during the first year after Benny's death. Well, the best-laid plans and all that. After yearning to get my life back to some type of ordinary, by absorbing the shock and replacing my pain with intimacy, I made the colossal decision to leave a job that I had spent the last ten years building. The life we had built in Michigan, the dreams we had, no longer fitted in with what needed to happen next in our newly formed family of two. I had been able to reach the height of my corporate career, in part because of Benny's love, support, and encouragement. He had not only slowed down his career advancement to enable me to work 50-hour weeks, travel the world and maintain a constant fire in my belly to succeed in a male-driven corporate world, he was also my biggest cheerleader! Benny played a significant part in the early stages of Jacob's development, as he took on the role of the primary caregiver. He allowed me the role of 'good cop', which helped ease my guilt over never being a very present mother.

He dished out the discipline, and I gave the gifts. Without him here to hold my hand, I had a decision to make. Do I have Jacob raised by a nanny while I try to go back to the life we had? Or do I give it all up, spend time getting to know my son, and be present for him as his only parent? The choice was made slightly simpler after my disastrous return to work earlier in May. I no longer wanted to be that version of myself. I was so grateful to the company that had opened doors of progression to me; the love they had shown me when Benny died is unforgettable, but it was time to leave. I resigned in September, and in December 2015, Jacob and I relocated back to the UK.

The first Christmas and New Year without Benny felt numb. Jacob and I smiled through it, and my family tried to make the best of a bad situation, which I adored them for. It was surreal to think that the year before, I was at home with my husband and son, baking cakes, opening gifts and enjoying the well-earned break curled up on the sofa, drinking wine and watching movies. The new reality was awful and with all ties severed from the life that I had built, disappearing into a rabbit hole of darkness and taking my son with me was my only desire. After many rounds of deliberation, I decided that the rabbit hole to hide in would be Barbados. In January 2016, Jacob and I left to spend six months in Barbados, where we could visit Benny's grave regularly, spend time healing with his family who knew our pain first-hand and, most importantly for me, be invisible from the world for a while. Not everyone has the luxury to go and hide on a Caribbean Island, and, to this day, I will be eternally grateful that I was in a financial position to take time out of life to be still. Did taking the year out have an impact on my future career? Of course. Did it have a long-term effect on my finances? Hell yes. I ended up exhausting all my savings and most of the life insurance that Benny had left. BUT... would I go back and change it? No way, because it changed the direction of my journey and, I would be so bold as to say, my life. Without that time, I would not have survived. I am also confident that I would not be here writing this book, hoping that it will help you as you walk your unique path of grief.

Arriving in Barbados I was blissfully unaware of how the next six months would impact my whole life. However, I felt instantly closer to Benny, and nine months after his death, I still had a burning desire to be where his body was. I knew that none of this was going to bring him back, but it gave me comfort to know that we were in the same place as his remains were. I never quite understood why people would visit the graves of those that had died so often, but I came to realise that, until you have lost someone you love, you cannot possibly empathise with what someone says or how someone acts to help them get through the pain. I can break down my six months in Barbados into three stages. The first is painful denial. My first prolonged period of anger would turn into the start of a rocky road to dependency on alcohol and marijuana and the first phase of acceptance that my husband had actually died and was never coming back. In my first few months in St Philip, the place that Benny called home, I visited his grave almost every day to feel closer to him. Some days the blistering heat would be unbearable, so I would not be able to stay long. Other days I would sit and just watch his grave, willing him to break open his coffin and fight his way through the dirt to come back to me. I would send messages to his Facebook messenger and WhatsApp telling him how much I missed him, hoping that he would send me a response. I'd listen to music and explain what new things Jacob was doing and ask his advice on how to handle certain situations. Isn't it funny how our minds have the capacity to try and rationalise the most unrealistic thoughts and scenarios when it is in a place of such desperation?

I'd wake up and rummage around for new ways to get through the day unscathed from feeling less heartache than the day before. Sex was currently not on the table as an outlet for comfort or escapism, so I replaced it with a new form of emotional support - alcohol. My thought process was that it would help me to do two things. One, it would anaesthetise me from the pain my heart was feeling. And two, it would help me sleep and enter into a temporary state of self-induced amnesia, praying that every time I closed my eyes, he would visit me in my dreams. Those initial moments when I would wake up from sleep and be unaware of the emotional warzone, I was living in were indescribable feelings of peace. And although I could forget how hollow my life felt for an instant, the fundamental flaw in my plan to drink my way out of loneliness always came with the reality that I was still a widow, Jacob still had no daddy, and I ended up feeling ten times worse. The wounds of shame and guilt superseded the bitter aftertaste of alcohol. Time and again, taking me back once again to the dependency cycle, I introduced you to in chapter three and experienced for the previous two chapters.

Rum was my drink of choice. And during the darkest stretch, I would get through about a half-litre a day. I chased it with cola or juice, and I drank little and often throughout the day so that the buzz would be gradual and last longer. As my dependency on alcohol grew, I knew that I would arouse suspicion if I started to drink larger quantities, but my body was becoming acclimated to drinking daily. As with most forms of dependency, I needed a more intense sensation and moved on to smoking weed (marijuana). I discovered that if I alternated smoking weed with drinking rum, I could remain in a blissfully euphoric state of mind that still allowed me to function undetected from my intensifying dependency. I had created a carefully structured routine around Jacob's daily school life, and other people's work lives. In Jacob's very early years, Benny's father had made sure that we acquired Jacobs's Barbados citizenship. With this in place, my mother-in-law had been able to secure a place at the local school for the duration of our six-month stay. I would drop him off at school, then come home or go to the beach, drink until about midday and sleep for a couple of hours before collecting him from school. I had no car throughout these times, so I would either catch the bus to collect him, or a family member would take me. Between the hours of 3:30 pm and his bedtime, I would be on mum duty, acting happy, doing homework, making dinner and playing my role. Jacob's bedtime was 7:30 pm; fortunately for me, he would always go straight to sleep, which meant I could go for my evening walk to the unfinished house Benny had been building. It was about a 1-minute walk from the main house but was far enough for me not to visit unnoticed. Throughout the next couple of hours, I would disappear into this make-believe world where I'd smoke weed, talk with his ghost and pretend that my life had not been broken into a million pieces. It was the time that I looked forward to most all day.

This pattern of slow cancerous destruction and the time I spent in my make-believe world was the perfect coping mechanism and my way of managing my grief. But we must also address the elephant in the room - the glaringly obvious fact was that I was becoming more and more dependent on alcohol and marijuana to get me through the day and night during this time. I was in an entire, enchanted state of denial, where I was dressing up my dependency as a vital source of comfort & survival. It was a ticking time bomb.

Painful Denial

One morning my sister-in-law, who would typically spend time in her room or the garden, decided to remain in the front of the house all morning. I remember sitting on my bed starting to get very agitated as that day the rum was in the kitchen and not in my room. I would ordinarily get a glass of coke or juice, take it to my room, and add the rum there to not arouse suspicion. But it was 9:30 am, and there was no plausible way to explain why I needed to drink rum and juice first thing in the morning. It was too exposed for me to smoke at the back of the house. And even if I could smoke, it was not the routine. I had a routine! The more time went on, the more agitated I got. "I couldn't have a drink; I couldn't have a drink, I couldn't have a drink", oh my goodness! In that small but significant moment, a voice inside my head spoke to me and said, "do you really need that drink, Alisa?" I remember looking at myself in the mirror, thinking, oh my goodness...I need a drink to get me through the day. Looking at my reflection in the mirror for what seemed a long time. I had an out of body experience that felt like I had been teleported into the future and back again in one split second. In that second, I could see what both mine and Jacob's future would look like if continuous drinking became my reality. I know it might sound unbelievable, but I believe that the little voice I heard was Jesus and what followed as a premonition of what things could look like for our future. I have come to realise that this is how Jesus works. He can show you what the choices you make can lead to, and in those moments, you have to decide. The life he showed me in that premonition made me want to choose a hopeful life for myself and my son, so that was the day my denial began to end, and the reality of my situation started to kick in. I would continue my battle with alcohol dependency over the years ahead, but I chose to have faith that things could feel better and was determined to be guided by Jesus to help heal me rather than continue to numb the pain with rum.

During this period of denial, the destruction affected me and impacted those close enough to see what was happening to me. I fooled myself into thinking that Jacob, who at that time was five years old, was oblivious to it. School time gave me the perfect window to grieve during the hours of 9 am and 3 pm. I thought I was hiding my sadness like a clever disguise. Little did I know that children see through the smoke and mirrors. Regardless of how well we may think we are shielding them, they sense when all is not well. In my case, Jacob mirrored and internalised his feelings, in the same way

I showed him, sabotaging our healing. A piece of advice; children will learn how to process and express their grief through seeing how and what you do. Don't be afraid to cry or express your feelings so that they know how to do the same. Otherwise, all you are teaching them to do is to internalise that which hurts them, which could set them up for a lifetime of emotional detachment.

First Dance with Anger

Denial was followed rapidly by anger. It snuck up on me like a thief in the night, burning this slow yet deliberate hole inside my heart. It wasn't the first time that I had felt anger, but it was the first time I had allowed it to seep into my pores. I started to ask myself some very poignant questions. Who was I angry at? Some days, I was mad at Jesus for taking him away from me. Sometimes and very often, I was mad at Benny for leaving us. I felt that if he had taken the medications that the doctors prescribed, he would still have been alive. Most of the time, though, I was angry at myself. I felt guilty for all the things I should have said, didn't say, or could have done differently. All the times I put my career advancement ahead of prioritising our marriage. The times that I felt his asthma was an inconvenience we could all do without as a family; the time I forgot my coat, and he gave me his, which led to him becoming sick; the list goes on and on. The longer I allowed this anger to consume me, the more it turned into behaviours that sabotaged myself and my close relationships with people I now felt nothing for but jealousy. Jealousy for family and friends who still had their husbands or partners to love them, be their cheerleaders, and be a father to their children. They could still carry on living the life that I once had. I had replaced my dependence on alcohol and marijuana with jealousy and hate. In my pursuit of vengeance for the life I had lost, for my husband, for Jacob's father, my career, the future we should have had, I made some deplorable choices! I cared for nothing other than wanting and longing to feel loved in whatever way felt right to me. I started a brief affair with someone very close to Benny. Looking back on it, I just wanted the most comparable replacement to him I could find. I didn't even think or care about the fact that he had a long-term partner, who had only ever been kind to me and classed me as a friend. The relationship lasted no more than a couple of months and was filled with the intensity and passion that reminded me so much of the early months of Benny and me when we first met in Barbados. Unbeknown to this man, I was re-enacting all the moments that I had lived and experienced with Benny to numb the pain and bring me closer to what I had lost. I would be lying if I told you that I didn't enjoy the time we spent together. I would also be lying if I told you that what we shared in those short months was all built on a lie. Because the truth be told, he is a wonderful person with a beautiful and creative mind, but in all sincerity, I think we were both trying to feel closer to Benny by being close to each other. I wouldn't go back and change a lot through my grief to glory journey as it has made me the woman I have become, but there are some events during these periods that I would love to go back and rewrite. In the absence of that. I want to say I'm sorry from the bottom of my heart for the hurt I caused, consciously and unconsciously, to my friends and family, but especially to a woman that only ever showed me love and friendship. I can't erase it or excuse it, but please know that I am deeply sorry for it. I have forgiven myself, and I hope you can forgive me too.

First Stage of Acceptance

After four months of the painful denial, anger phase, I was exhausted by a cycle of destruction. I came to a standstill and realised that my life had to move in a different direction. I had to admit that the plan for my future no longer involved being married to this incredible man. I had to accept he was dead. It was an endless puzzling journey where the goal of admission seemed completely unachievable at times. I also made the mistake of thinking I was healed from it all after this first acceptance phase and was so disappointed when it happened repeatedly. I went on to have several more 'acceptance' phases before I reached the place where I could return to a meaningful place in my life. It is so important to remind yourself that it is normal to go through one stage of the grief cycle many times and not to feel like you have gone backwards in your healing because of it. Admitting that my life would never be the same again was such an excruciating transition from the reluctant participative approach to life that I had been sustaining for the previous 12 months since his death. I was in a tug of war with having to stand still and face the absoluteness of my reality and the desire to run and hide into my make-believe world any chance I could get. In the end, the only place I felt I could go to get guidance and to speak out my pain was with Jesus. I pleaded with him to take away the agony and help me understand what my next steps should be. I did not get on my knees and pray daily; it started with a simple everyday dialogue. I told him the pain that I was in and that I wanted to change my life, and could he show me a way forward.

The first thing that became clear was that getting my mind, body, and soul in sync was an essential step in my healing. I wanted to learn more about health and fitness benefits during the grief process, so I decided to take an online course and studied fitness and nutrition. This helped me to understand the right balance of how to train and fuel my body with the right endorphins, nutrients and vitamins for healing. I was navigated to a constant flow of spiritual connection and guidance through gospel and worship music that inspired me to get up at 5:00 am to train at the backyard gym, where Benny had started his love affair with weight training many years before. This music also became the playlist that would become the backdrop to a spiritual skipping workout program I designed that kept me occupied in the evenings after Jacob had gone to sleep; no more smoking, just skipping! Watch this space, as Jesus wants me to launch this one day! He also introduced me to Elevation Church; the sermons from Pastor Steven Furtick enabled the Holy Spirit to turn my spiritual light on. This was the catalyst that helped me read and take comfort from the Bible.

I spoke about this in an earlier chapter. The five stages of grief are necessary. It hurts like hell, and you may become dependent on any manner of things to try and numb the pain of loss. Through my experience, I would encourage you to try your hardest not to run away from the emotional numbness or try to feel something by becoming dependent on things that will physically or emotionally harm you. Can I say that I would not have gone through this period of darkness had I spoken to somebody sooner? No, I can't. But I'm grateful for my faith in Jesus, my relationships with my loved ones, and especially my son, as these all gave me the strength to realise that the choices, I was making weren't the right path for me. Also, as I have mentioned several times, the sooner you can speak to a professional to help you understand your feelings and find healthy coping mechanisms, the more minor potential damage you will do to yourself and those you love.

CHAPTER 7

THE SEASON OF SADNESS

My Return to the UK

After pondering for a long time on where Jacob and I should set up our new life, I decided, with reluctance, that the best place for us was with my Mum and Dad in Coventry. The reluctance did not come from not wanting to be with my parents; it was quite the opposite. I was looking forward to spending time with them. My Mum had told me she felt obsolete over the past year. She had been distraught that she could not get to Michigan when Benny died. She and my father had pawned jewellery just so that she had enough for a plane ticket, but the problem came from the long process of getting a US visa, as she doesn't have a British passport. In any case, I felt it was more important for her to be with me at the funeral in Barbados. When she finally arrived, I believe that she expected that she would be able to make everything better for me, what mother wouldn't. The only problem was that I was wrapped up in the crippling feelings of grief and guilt about bringing Benny back to his family in a box that I had no time to spend with her. Then in the four weeks when Jacob and I had spent time in the UK before we left in early 2016 to stay in Barbados for six months, I had opted to stay anywhere but at her house. In preparation for this book, my mum revealed that she felt that I didn't want or need her, which was so far from the truth. The reluctance to stay with her came from two things that were at odds in my mind. One was that Benny and I had lived at her house for 90% of our time before moving to the US, so you see, it wasn't my parent's home I couldn't face; it was the memories we created there. The house was filled with his scent and footprint. In every corner, a reminder of the gaping hole he had left behind. Secondly, my mum knows me better than anyone in the world and would have seen straight through my facade of 'the strong widow who is coping'.

The Room with a View

The feeling of failure, dread, and uncertainty of what lay ahead of me was so overwhelming! I had returned to the UK from Barbados with a spring in my step. I was filled with optimism and thinking that the 'first acceptance' stage of the grief cycle meant that I had been healed from my grief. Laughable, I know, but I truly believed that I was okay and ready to start my life over. It was now July of 2016, and a little over a year had passed since Benny's death. The time had flown by, yet there were so many feelings that made everything feel like he had just died. I found myself looking out of what used to be my bedroom window when I was growing up. The same window that I looked out of when I dreamed of being a singing superstar at eleven. The window I had looked out of after receiving disappointing GCSE results. The window where I sat and cried after my first boyfriend broke my heart. The window where Benny and I looked out of whilst talking about what we planned to do with our lives together. The window that I had looked out of whilst rocking Jacob back to sleep again during his first months in this world. And now the window I was looking out of as a widow. Standing, glaring out of that window, made me feel like such a failure. How could I be back here again?! I had worked so hard on my career. I had met and married an incredible man and had a beautiful son. I was promoted and moved to the USA, had a condo by the lake, drove a Range Rover, and earned a six-figure salary. I had what I felt was a perfect life. What had I done wrong to get me back here looking out of this window? An even bigger question was, what in the world was I supposed to do next?

After returning home to my parents, I found myself speaking with Jesus every minute of every day for quite a while. My internal dialogue with him centred on why, how, when, what questions. Why am I back here? How can I go on? When will this stop hurting? What should I do next for a job? With these questions on a daily speed play loop in my mind, I felt like I was descending into a pit of confusion and felt powerless to say anything to my family. My annoyance towards them only exacerbated my desire to show them how strong I was. I had convinced myself that their expectation of me was the same as my desire to appear like I had it all together. Little did I know that through my painted-on smile and my very rehearsed line of, "I'm okay, everything is fine", they all knew I wasn't but felt helpless to make it better for either me or Jacob. How could they help me when I didn't even know how I could help myself? I was infuriated that even though it had been a year and a half, to me, it felt like yesterday, and everybody else was getting on with their lives. Everybody else seemed to be happy. Everybody else seemed to have plans for their future, while I was left wedged in the past, breathing the oxygen of memories and tragedy that never seemed to fill my lungs with enough clean air. It was so painful, not wanting to look back, not wanting to look forward. It was official - I was stranded in the middle of no man's land.

As you can imagine, the spring in my step I had felt in Barbados had now become a slow, lifeless walk that rapidly turned into a complete feeling of numbness. So much so that for almost six months, I felt like a zombie. I tried to pretend that everything was okay, but my relationships with those closest to me were completely falling apart! And like a steam train travelling at high speed, I found myself heading back to the grief stage of anger. This time around, it was even more sinister and cold. I knew that if I did not get it under control, some relationships would not survive the after-effects. The problem I was about to learn was that you could not control anger during grief. You cannot contain or tame it. You have to face it head-on, look it square in the eyes and confront it. What I needed to figure out, though, was how on earth could I do this while being right in the middle of extreme pain.

In The Barren Land

The Collins dictionary definition of the word helpless is:

- *Unable to manage independently.*
- *Made powerless or weak.*
- *Without help*

If you were to read these three definitions over and over and over again, it could start to make you feel very negative. And what does negativity spawn? Yes, you guessed it - more negativity. This mentality can and usually will take you on a reluctantly inevitable journey into a murky state of mind. I felt like my body had been temporarily immobilised at the same time as losing the power of speech, all the while my mind consciously kicking, screaming, and fighting to regain mobility. However, the longer I was unable to speak or move, the quieter my mind became. The silence turned into loneliness and anxiety, which isolated me from the world. Internalising my feelings of helplessness and negativity about my future then became my daily battle. The performance of smiling and pretending I was okay began to feel like I was wearing a heavy yet invisible cloak of gloom that felt more and more like a straightjacket the longer it stayed on me. It had crept up on me and arrived so quietly and unassumingly; the all-consuming D-word ... Depression. And just like in the nursery rhyme Humpty Dumpty, I fell off the wall. I'd crumbled into a million broken pieces and felt that all the king's horses and all the king's men would never be able to put me back together again.

Three years had now passed since Benny's death. The thought of depression being something that I was suffering from hit me like a tonne of bricks. I was so unprepared for the enormity of the stage of my journey that lay ahead. A season of sadness which was a continuous heavy load bearing down on my shoulders. A desolate, empty void of loneliness. I was lost! There were moments where the hurt was so intolerable, I could physically feel it in my body. Have you ever felt like your soul was being punched so hard and persistently that it made your body ache? Well, that is the type of pain I was in, and it crippled me to the core. I was alone, a single parent with my career in tatters. Financially I was struggling and, for the first time in my life, I couldn't see a way out; no light at the end of any tunnel. I was desperate and in despair. I wanted to die. I am not ashamed to tell you that there were moments during my most profound hurt when I had thoughts and plans to end Jacob and my life. Moments when I felt there was no reason to be here. The pain of loss and grief dragged my legs down into the quicksand of despair. I am not ashamed to tell you this because I know that anyone who has felt loss in such a profound way can go through this stage. I don't want to sidestep such an essential area in my grief journey for fear of how people may see or judge me. I still had to force myself to get up every day and make the first couple of hours somewhat lighter to give Jacob some sense of stability. I had taken a backward step in my career, and though I was grateful to have a job that gave me a salary, it was a middle management role, where I was travelling every day, which gave me no time for anything other than working and sleeping. I hated it with a passion. I was also still pretending, for the most part, that I was moving forward in my grief journey when I really felt like I was taking one step back every single day.

We were now living in a new house. After the busyness of the day had ended and Jacob was in his bed, all I had for company were my two new best friends: loneliness and fear. And right on cue, they brought with them my old comfort blankets of alcohol and marijuana. I was now deep into my desolate and barren land. No water, no light, just nothingness. I was desperate to feel something, and for a short while, it felt like Jesus could not fill that void. I had started to question whether He was ever going to get me out of my daily pursuit of happiness. When was the darkness going to turn into the light? When would it be time to feel continuous bouts of joy? I missed my husband's physical presence, his smile, his smell, his voice! I missed the way he always kissed me when he came home, the way he always told me that I looked nice... every day! I missed the way he always opened the car door for me and made sure that I walked on the inside of the pavement. I missed the way he touched, kissed and made love to me, sometimes gently and sometimes with a raw desire to own every part of me. I missed our arguments and how he would get vexed with me but keep his cool while I went off on a tirade of rants and raves. When provoked, I missed how he would defend and protect those he loved; his gentle giant nature would turn into the incredible hulk. I missed his love for Jesus and his ability to make all those he met feel at ease. He was always genuinely interested in learning more about people and their lives. I missed his ambition to better himself and our lives by pursuing his love of art. I MISSED HIM! Yet in and amongst missing him, I was furious with him. He always promised that he would never leave me, but he did. Even though he had been hospitalised several times before with his asthma. His desire to treat it naturally infuriated me. I had got him to see an asthma specialist in the UK and an Ears, Nose & Throat specialist in the US. It made no difference. No matter what they told him or prescribed, he knew better.

I have said repeatedly that the importance of understanding that the stages of grief do not follow any particular order cannot be underestimated. Well, I was now in the depression and anger stage all at the same time. Add to the mix my feeling of lifelessness, missing the physical presence of my husband's touch, loneliness, and fear of my reliance on alcohol and marijuana... What does that equal? A full-on mental breakdown. I was all out of everything! Trying to deal with the symptoms rather than the root cause of my pain aggravated my breakdown even more. It was time to go to the doctor. I went looking for support and guidance, but all he did was happily and easily supply me with Amitriptyline, a form of antidepressant. I remember being on it for about two weeks and telling my mother how terrible it made me feel in the mornings. She told me that it was better to take them earlier in the evening, around 7 pm. The next day we were at her house, and Jacob came rushing downstairs utterly distressed. With his voice trembling with concern, he told me we needed to go home. When I asked him why he replied, "Mummy, you need to get home to take your tablets, remember?" That's the moment I said goodbye to Amitriptyline.

CHAPTER 8

FINDING MY WAY BACK TO HIM

Who Is God, Jesus and The Holy Spirit

Before I delve into my faith, let me provide you with some basic knowledge. Having a relationship with God and having a relationship with Jesus are two important concepts that are often talked about. God is the creator of everything and the ultimate authority in the universe. Having a relationship with God means acknowledging his existence and recognising that we are made in his image, and he has a plan for our lives. However, there is another figure named Lucifer who wanted to challenge God's power. Lucifer is a fallen angel who rebelled against God and was cast out of heaven and is also known as Satan or the Devil. He persuaded the first humans, Adam and Eve, to disobey God, which resulted in the introduction of sin into the world. Sin is doing something that is wrong or bad. It's like breaking the rules, but on a bigger level. It's doing things that hurt ourselves, others, or God. As Christians we believe that everyone is born with a sinful nature, which means we're not perfect and we make mistakes. The Bible teaches us that continued sin separates us from God and can lead to bad consequences in our lives. But the good news is that we also believe in forgiveness and second chances.

As Christians we also believe in the concept of free will, which means that we have the ability to make our own choices in life. We can choose to follow God and live a good life or go our own way, which may lead us to trouble. Despite our human flaws, God loves us unconditionally and as such He sent his son, Jesus. Jesus is the son of God who came to earth in human form to save humanity from sin and to show us how to live a life filled with love, kindness, and compassion. Jesus was a person who reached out to the marginalised and preached unity for all people, regardless of race, gender, or social status. Unfortunately, not everyone accepted Jesus, and he was persecuted and killed. But the amazing part is that he rose from the dead three days later, which is why as Christians we believe in eternal life. By believing in Jesus and striving to live our lives as he did, we can join him in heaven when we die. As Christians we believe that by asking God to forgive us for our sin filled lives. By accepting that Jesus came to earth as our personal saviour and who showed us the right example of how to live. By giving His life to save ours and by rising again showing that we will have a life with God even after we die. We can be forgiven, have a fresh start, be given a clean slate like being 'born again'.

Another crucial concept in Christianity is the Holy Spirit, which is God's presence that lives within us. The Holy Spirit bestows upon us special gifts, to help us fulfil our purpose in life.

The bible tells us that:

God's various gifts are handed out everywhere; but they all originate in God's Spirit. God's various ministries are carried out everywhere;

but they all originate in God's Spirit. God's various expressions of
power are in action everywhere; but God himself is behind it all.
Each person is given something to do that shows who God is:
Everyone gets in on it, everyone benefits. All kinds of things are
handed out by the Spirit, and to all kinds of people! The variety is
wonderful: wise counsel, clear understanding, simple trust, healing the
sick, miraculous acts, proclamation, distinguishing between spirits,
tongues (a spiritual language), interpretation of tongues. All these
gifts have a common origin but are handed out one by one by the one
Spirit of God. He decides who gets what, and when.
1 Corinthians 12:8-11 (The Message Translation)

In summary, Christianity is about love and hope. God loves
us, and Jesus showed us how to love others. The Holy Spirit
helps us spread that love throughout the world. If you want
to learn more about Christianity, then head to my website
justcallmealisa.com.

What Does Having Hope and Faith Really Mean

Believing in God does not make us exempt from challenging
times or situations but believing in Him even through those
times demonstrates our level of trust that He knows the plan
for our life, and he has also created us with all the qualities
and spiritual gifts needed to survive 'Life'. But again, it's our
choice to decide to trust Him and have faith and hope in
Him and His plan for our lives even if we cannot see how He
will get us there. I am not going to lie to you though, in times
of deep-pain and sorrow I have struggled to see that hope
and have faith.

One thing I continue to look at is what the word faith actually means; not to everyone else but to me. The dictionary has several meanings but the one I like the most is; 'To have great trust or confidence in something or someone.' However, if we look at the Hebrew origins of the word faith we trace it back to a word called Emunah (Eh – moo – nah). Now the word Emunah does mean to have faith, but it has a broader meaning that has implications for what God calls us to as people of faith. It contains the idea of steadfastness or persistence. In the bible it says in the book of Hebrews chapter 11 verse 1, *'Faith is the confidence that what we hope for will actually happen; it gives us assurance about things we cannot see.'* One of the examples of having steadfast faith is a story in a bible that I love and it's about a woman who had suffered with continuous bleeding for twelve long, agonising years. During biblical times, women who experienced abnormal bleeding were considered ritually unclean and were not allowed to take part in religious ceremonies or be in public spaces. This meant that she would have been ostracised from her community and would have felt isolated and ashamed. In addition, the condition she had would have caused her physical pain and discomfort. She would have felt weak, dizzy, and fatigued from the loss of blood. It's likely that her chronic condition would have also caused her emotional pain and stress as she struggled with her illness and the societal stigma that came with it. She would have had no family, no friends, no money and in fact she would have had every right to be angry and bitter. Despite all of this, her level of faith and determination is awe inspiring to me. She believed that if she could just touch Jesus' clothes, she would be healed. Her story is truly inspiring and serves as a reminder of the incredible strength that can come from faith. It's a powerful example of how, even in the darkest of times, we can find hope and light in the belief that there is something greater than ourselves guiding our path. It's a message that we all need to hear, and one that can help us navigate life's challenges with grace and resilience.

I will be very honest, when I gave my life to Christ three days after Benny died, he gave me a choice which was clear and hopeful. But the three years that followed when I was in the eye of my storm, and I was putting my hope and faith in everything other than in Him led me further and further away from the promise that he gave to me. Maybe you are in a place right now where you're struggling to see how you are going to move out of a place of pain, grief or deep loss. Or perhaps you are in a place full of sadness, confusion when being around family, friends or people whose lives are continuing whilst yours is in the wake of devastation is leaving you feeling bitter or angry. Or maybe you're tired of pretending that you're ok, smiling externally whilst being in excruciating agony on the inside and you feel alone.

Let me tell you something: in my journey I have learnt that God's steadfast love and mercy is immovable, and hope can be found in the middle of our sorrow, but we have to have the type of biblical faith that is much more than just believing that things will get better. I had to live my life in full reliance upon Him. I had to make a decision, a choice, I had to have an Emunah level of faith.

God Never Moves, We Do!

I have the most incredible family and friends. Some of them knew that there was something desperately wrong with me, and they tried their very best to let me know they were there when I needed to offload the burden of my grief. They would immediately check in with me when they saw a cryptic social media post or change of profile pictures, showing me, Benny and Jacob in happier times, which were always secret cries for help. To say that I was and am blessed to have had this level of love around me is an understatement. They will truly never understand how many times they saved me from falling deeper into the abyss of depression and ending it all. But how could I tell everybody that I was feeling suicidal when I'd spent the best part of three years saying, with a painted smile on my face, "I'm fine," "everything is okay!" I said it so often I was even able to fool myself into believing that I was moving forward with my life in a successful way. I say all of that to say this. Regardless of the love and support I had around me, depression is like an uninvited and unwelcome guest at a dinner party. It takes over everything with its offensive and loud behaviour. Then dinner becomes breakfast. Breakfast becomes lunch, and before you know it, depression has moved into your home and is the worst house guest. The longer it stays with you, the harder it becomes to ask it to leave.

I have realised in my journey that God has and continues to show up in my life at critical times and in very unexpected ways. As I mentioned earlier, I felt that my relationship with Him was in a period of cool down. Not talking to Him daily and trying to do things in my strength and in my own way could not fill the void raging through my heart. The longer I distanced myself from Him, the more challenging things became. In my absence from Him, I tried to fill my emptiness with things that would never help me heal. The interesting lesson for me is that God never moves; we move away from Him. The more steps we take to fill our lives with temptations, distractions and anything that does not allow Him to guide our actions is what we call sin. The more we sin and lose faith and hope, the further away **we take ourselves** from feeling His love.

Picture an onion it has so many layers right. Well now imagine sin as one of those circular layers. The more we sin the more layers are created until we are so far away from feeling God's love. The thing is He has not stopped loving us but those barriers convince us that he no longer hears our cries of despair or pleas for help.

LIVING IN OUR OWN STENGTH

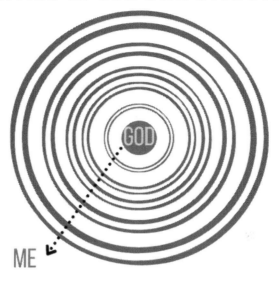

However, the most beautiful thing about God's love is this: We move, and He doesn't. The way back to Him is easy and immediate because His love is always there. He was the only one that was able to tell my unwelcome guest of depression to leave without fear or hesitation. The same one who enabled me to unchain myself from my dependency on alcohol and marijuana before it shackled me again. The same one who helped me understand that I needed to confront my anger before it took over and wreaked havoc on my relationships again. The same one that showed me my worth comes from more than being intimate with multiple men. Jesus stepped in again, but this time it was to save me from the ravages of my mind. There will be those wondering how God can speak to depression and ask it to leave. I can understand your possible scepticism so let me simplify it. I believe we all have the capability to bring ourselves out of a negative state of mind. All we have to do is look at how we communicate with children. When they fall and hurt themselves, what do we say to them? Do we say, 'Oh dear, you have fallen, well that is going to hurt for a long time, be prepared to have a scar there for the rest of your life to remind you of this moment that you will never get over? Suppose you have a teenager that has failed an important exam. Do you say, 'Oh dear, well you have failed, there is no point in thinking you will get into the university you wanted, you can kiss goodbye to that career, and without a job, you can't get any money, so no woman or man will want you, broke and with no prospects? Do you see where I am going with this? When we are younger, we are programmed to look on the bright side of life for the most part. We try to focus the attention of children and young people to see the positive outcomes of any situation. As adults, we can still tap into our childlike state of positive being. The reason we do not is that we allow life events to get in the way. And the more we fall over or fail a test, the more we remind ourselves to look on the negative side rather than the positive side. If you also have bad influences around, it can all seem even worse. Remember what I said earlier about negativity spawning negativity? Well, let's flip it and look at how positivity can spawn positivity.

Now, going back to how God told my depression to leave. As I said at the beginning of this chapter He is my father. Like any loving parent He wants only the best for my life. He gives me advice, steps into a situation and takes charge. He reminds me of my childlike instinct to trust him as a parent and listen to his guidance. He is always ready and waiting to hear from me. All I have to do is to ask Him for help. Help to overcome issues of loneliness and fear about the future. Help with finding better ways of dealing with my feelings of anger and frustration. Help to stop relying on toxic comfort blankets that take me further away from Him. And most importantly, help in letting go of my loss, grief and past so that I can start to live my life forward. He's always ready and waiting to welcome us back into His arms when we move far away from Him. In the parable of the lost sheep, we refer to Jesus as the shepherd and people as the sheep.

'Be happy with me because I found my lost sheep.' In the same way, I tell you there is more joy in heaven over one sinner who changes his heart and life, than over ninety-nine good people who don't need to change'
Luke 15:6-7 New Century Version

TRUSTING IN GOD

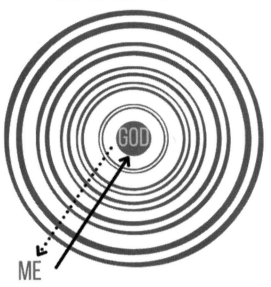

Unlike Humpty Dumpty, where all the king's horses and all the king's men couldn't put him back together again, I can tell you from experience that God has miraculous healing powers. The Bible tells us in Psalms 146 and 147 that he is a father to the fatherless, a defender of widows and that he heals the broken-hearted and binds up their wounds. Knowing His unconditional love for me enables me to dig deeper during my darkest moments and deepest despair. In these painful moments, my father has reminded me to do the only thing I know how to do, and that is to trust him, to speak with him in prayer and pray my way out of the darkness and follow his light. Whether you are a Christian or not, if you feel like now is a time you could use his help and guidance but don't know what to say. I want you just to sit where you are, take a deep breath and think about the issue you want to talk to Jesus about.

Once you've done this, and even if things feel hopeless, I want to encourage you to ask him for help and say, 'Jesus, I give my issues to you, help me to overcome them. Then read his response and what he tells us in the Bible.

'Fear not, for I am with you; be not dismayed, for I am your God. I will strengthen you, yes, I will help you, I will uphold you with My righteous right hand. For I, the LORD your God, will hold your right hand, saying to you, do not fear, I will help you.' - Isaiah 41:10 & 13.

CHAPTER 9

WHEN I CAME OUT OF THE WATER

Once upon a time, a boy met a girl on a train platform in Coventry. After exchanging numbers, they had a brief summer romance, which ended as quickly as it had started. The boy became a man, got married, then divorced. He had a successful career, found Christ, and dedicated his life to making others better. But throughout the years, he never forgot about the girl he met at the train station. As for the girl... well, you're reading part of her story right now. That girl is me.

Now, let's fast forward 15 years. I received a LinkedIn connection request from a man whose surname was the same as Benny's family name. After a few days passed I was scrolling through my Facebook messenger when I realised that this same man had sent me a friend request. I remember immediately wondering which part of Benny's family he fitted into and if I had ever met him before, but after accepting the request I thought nothing more of it. Then, several weeks later, he sent me a message on LinkedIn. I clicked onto his profile, thinking I would find out where the connection to Benny comes from. To my distress, we only had one mutual friend, and not with anyone in Benny's family; it was with a lady that I was working with at that time. As I investigated his profile further, it was evident to me that I had accepted a friend request from a guy that I did not actually know. Big sigh. His message read: -

---

Hi Alisa

So nearly 15 years ago I met the most amazing girl on a train with my friend going to Birmingham. We got to know each other little and just like she appeared she vanished again and I didn't even get her surname. Until she unexpectedly appears in my timeline all these years later.

You seem to be doing well and I'd love to hear more about what you've been up to all this time.
Regards

I remember being at my mother's house at the time he sent the message. I showed it to her and said, 'this is a bit weird, isn't it?' Since getting over my breakdown, my mum and other family members were getting a little worried about the fact that I did not seem interested in dating. I'm certain she thought that this was the perfect opportunity to get me back in the game. I also believe there was a genuine desire to see me smile again with a man. Almost certainly with all this in mind, my mum replied, "I think it is quite romantic, why don't you respond? It would be good for you to make a new friend". I screwed my nose up and thought, 'yeah, right.' I was not going to message back. Why would I?

My 'why would I' soon turned into 'well why wouldn't I?' He was not saying he wanted to marry me, for goodness sake. Thinking back and remembering the short romance we had and the fact that it was 15 years later, I decided to respond. It was the polite thing to do, right?

Alisa Harewood · 1:02 AM

Omggggg I remember now 🔫 I am so sorry I haven't responded sooner. My goodness it has been a very long time ago... wowwww

Then without thinking...

Alisa Harewood · 1:03 AM

How are you doing, I am well... a lifetime has passed since then. We should connect and catch up. My number ████████████ what's app me when you get a chance.

Wow! I had sent him my number.

Why did I do that?!!! I tried to figure out how to delete it from LinkedIn, but before I could figure that out, he had messaged me back. Eeeekkkk! After a series of message exchanges and within a couple of days, we had our first date.

The following six months were a whirlwind of emotions for both of us. I was unexpectedly falling in love. The journey to that point had not been easy, but he opened me up again, and I felt alive and happy. This beautifully exciting feeling was also tinged with a sense of anxiety and fear. I went in and out of thinking I deserved this, at the same time feeling like I was cheating on a ghost. By month 8, we got engaged. I was so happy and relieved to know that I could feel love and be loved again. However, weaved into the joy of this new love we were creating were the scars of my grief journey. It was like I was running forward in slow motion with my past pulling me back, saying no, it's not time to move on yet. It's not time for you to be happy. Even though I felt ready for the new, something was stopping me.

FEAR | False Evidence Appearing Real

The problem with fear is that it has so many variables. During this season of knowing, I wanted to move forward but didn't have enough strength to stop my anxiety from controlling the narrative of my life. Fear crippled me. Anytime I took a step towards the grief stage of acceptance, fear pulled me back by the neck and strangled my hope. As a result, I did not know how to enjoy and be present in the moment. I was allowing the past to disrupt my present, sabotaging moments of peace and ruining moments of joy. I was allowing the memory of my past loss to consume me and stop me from looking too far forward. I had to stop holding on to my fear of letting go, as I knew I was ready to move forward. With my fiancé being a man of God, he encouraged me to develop my relationship with the Lord at a deeper level. I was growing, and I knew that if I was going to overcome my fear, I needed to let go and let God guide my every step. It was time to make a public declaration and say goodbye to my past and to my fear. It was time to get baptised!

At this time, it had been four years since I had given my life to Christ amid my tragedy. God has called me according to the potential He knows I have. He knew I was a fighter because that is who He created me to be. And He knows you are too. Believe that you are capable of digging deeper than you ever have done before and tapping into that childlike voice that says, 'I CAN' rather than 'I CAN'T'. He is perfectly okay with the space between who you are now and who he knows you will become. He sees the fighter in you! You will never truly feel ready to let go of your fear, but God will prepare and bring things into your life to enable you to push past your fears and continue to take one step at a time. The question becomes how big or small do you want your steps to be?

Baptism was not something I had felt I needed to do, until I reached a point when being washed anew was the only way I could see myself finally getting rid of the dark cloud that seemed to be following me. Even though I felt that I had moved on, there seemed to be some invisible weight pulling me back all the time and it did not feel like the grip or the remains of grief. It felt like a deeper wound, something that was hidden and that had been locked away. I remember praying and talking with God the night before my baptism. We both knew it was time for me to leave it all in the water. I felt that the time to move into my purpose needed to start with the unbreaking of any chains that were holding me back.

All the important people in my life had travelled to my home church in Coventry. The day had come, and I felt ready—no feelings of anxiety, only a sense that this was the day that everything would change. The main service had been powerful, and as I made my way to change into my baptism clothes in the bathroom, I took a moment to think about how far God had brought me since 2015. He had carried me through all the pain of the first couple of months after I lost Benny and my heart was broken into a million pieces; all the various stages of anger, depression, loneliness, and fear during the years that followed: the overcoming of my dependency to sex, alcohol and marijuana, rather than letting it rule me and rob me of my sense of joy; the moments where I felt like I would never feel anything again and the times where dying and ending it all seemed like the only way out of my grief. I tearfully looked at myself in the mirror, and with a sense of indescribable gratitude, I said a prayer that went something like this.

'God, thank you for bringing me to this place. I am so grateful for all the lessons you have taught me in preparation for what is next. I ask of you on this day that it be the day I leave everything in the water! Let my past be the past! Let me be washed anew! Let the chains of grief be broken, and let me step into a new chapter of my Life without FEAR! When I come out of the water Lord, reveal anything that has been holding me back consciously or subconsciously. No longer allow these things to stop me from moving into the purpose you have laid out for my life. Today is the day, and the time is now. I am ready!!!!

If you do not face your fears and accept that it is an essential and integral part of the grief journey, it will do one of two things. It will either distract you or destroy you. For me, those distractions came in the form of addictions and comfort blankets which, if left unchecked, I do not doubt would have led to the destruction of my life; snowballing into generational trauma which could have had a life-changing impact on my son's life, his children's lives, and so the circle of life would go on with ancestral chains bound together through the pain and hurt that started with the trauma and fear that I could not accept and move past.

Overcoming the fear of moving forward is not something that I have been able to do in isolation; in fact, I have had to put all my faith in God. God knew the journey He was taking me on. He tells us in Jeremiah 1:5 that, "Before I formed you in the womb I knew you, before you were born, I set you **apart."**

FEAR = Forget Everything And Rise.

Fear now has a new meaning in my life, and I pray that it will for you: Forget Everything and Rise. God will reward you for stepping out of fear and into faith. A perfect example of that is, remember that man that I spoke about at the beginning of this chapter, that man that I met many many many years ago on the train platform before this tragedy ever happened to me, the same man that encouraged me to get baptised and deepen my relationship with God. The same man that has stuck by my side and had faith when I did not. The same man that has watched and played a part in Jacob's life, well that ladies and gentlemen is the same man that I went on to marry.

Don't let fear stop you from moving forward into a brand-new life a life that is waiting for you on the other side of that pain. Carlyle helped me to visualise my future. A future that

I wanted to be filled with joy, with love, with light, with faith, with purpose. Don't let fear or guilt stop you from being happy. Your life did not end and has not ended, you deserve to be happy and whole. Forgetting everything and rising does not mean that you forget about the person you have lost but it does mean that you have decided to put yourself and your happiness first so that you can find joy.

CHAPTER 10

THE HEALING SEASON

It's Your Turn Now

In a devotional book that I was reading at the time, 'Grieving Jesus's Way - A 90-day devotional' by Margaret Brownley, there is a section where it talks about understanding that the loss of the person, we love is not the only loss that comes from death. Understanding these additional areas of loss may help you as you start the journey to grieve for the associated impact of all that you have lost, not just the person. I can tell you that it gave me a greater insight into the enormous extent to which Benny's death set off a chain reaction of loss in areas that I would later come to realise were the end of specific chapters of my life but the beginning of others. Letting go usually involves some form of forgiveness or acceptance - whether it's yourself, someone else, a situation or even an unknown third party. The learning and irony are that whatever we are holding onto - it's probably hurting or bothering you more than anyone else.

Although the impact on those you love could be felt far and wide. These things we hold onto, like grudges, anger or hurt, cloud our minds and prevent us from being the best we can be.

Although the impact on those you love could be felt far and wide. These things we hold onto, like grudges, anger or hurt, cloud our minds and prevent us from being the best we can be. Letting go doesn't mean we forgot about what has happened. It's about lightening OUR load, setting ourselves free and reclaiming our energy so that we can live our lives looking forward and not backwards.

I did an exercise and have revisited it at various stages of my grief journey. It has been interesting to see how Benny's death impacted so many areas of my life. I will also ask you to do some reflective writing, so have a pen and pad or smartphone handy to make notes. I will warn you this is not an easy exercise to do, so if you do not feel ready, it's okay; you can come back to it when you feel ready. On the other hand, if you feel prepared to ask yourself the question 'What do I need to do to allow me to let go', let's begin...

PART ONE

Whilst you may not wish to do anything about this right now, just listing what you need to let go of here will raise your level of awareness, and you'll naturally begin to loosen your grip. Be in a quiet place where you can spend some uninterrupted time thinking about all the areas you are holding onto. What slows you down, what takes you back to unhealthy habits and anything that gets in the way of you moving forward.

Now list below the top 5 things that you need to let go of.

1.

2.

3.

4.

5.

PART TWO

Now spend time thinking about how you, your family and friends and life benefit from holding on to these things? If you struggle with identifying a benefit (there must be something you can think of, or you wouldn't be holding on to it). Ask yourself, "What do I gain by keeping hold of this?" Perhaps holding onto the loss, resentment, anger, or hurt stops you from accepting that your life has changed, and that the person is no longer here.

Now for each thing, you want to let go of, list at least one way you benefit from holding onto it.

1.

2.

3.

4.

5.

PART THREE

I would like you to make sure for this part of the exercise; you are sitting in a place that you feel comfortable and relaxed; we will do a five-minute mindfulness exercise so that you can feel prepared for the next part of the exercise.
NB: This section is also available for you to do as a guided meditation on my YouTube channel @justcallmealisa.

I'd like you to get comfortable in your chair. Take a deep breath in and out and place your feet flat on the floor, really FEELING your feet in contact with the ground underneath you. And just take a few more deep breaths in and out for about 30 seconds or until you feel relaxed [pause].

- So, I'd like you to start by focusing on your toes. Scrunch them up, and then release. [pause] Now relax your ankles [pause], calf muscles [pause], knees [pause] and thigh muscles [pause]. Let any thoughts you may have float up and away from you in an air bubble. [pause]. Now relax your buttocks [pause], pelvic area [pause] and begin to notice any tension you may have in your back. Breathe deeply in, and as you breathe out, slowly relax and release any tension you may have in your back. [pause] Now your shoulders. Lift them up and then release them completely. Wonderful. [pause] Now it's time to relax your neck and jaw muscles. Take a deep breath in, and as you breathe out let go of any tension you're holding in your neck and jaw [pause]. Relax the top of

132

your head [pause], let all the tension flow up into the air.

- Now I want you to visualise the five things that you need to let go of and imagine letting go of everything in this list. Take a deep breath in and out and with every breath out, let go of one thing at a time. See that thing disappear into the air, or shatter into a million pieces, like a pane of glass. Do this as many times as you feel that you need to, but the objective is to make a conscious decision to let go of things that you are holding onto and that are stopping you from moving forward.

- Take a few more deep breaths and enjoy this feeling of letting go for a little while longer. [longer pause about 1 minute]

- I'd like you to now slowly bring your attention back to the room. Begin noticing the sounds around you, the smell of things around you, feel your feet on the floor, bring yourself back to a place of being in the moment and when you're ready, slowly open your eyes [pause].

Take a moment to write down all the things you are feeling, what have you learned about yourself from doing this exercise. If you think of fear, anxiety, pain, depression or worry, do not feel disheartened. Take some time and revisit this exercise at a different time.

NOTES

You don't need to know HOW to let go; you just need to be WILLING to want to let go. You can't change the past, you can't bring back all the things you have lost, but you can learn from it and change how you feel going forward. And remember, whatever you find the hardest to let go of is probably what you need to let go of the most. However, I am hopeful that you felt joy, happiness, positivity, freedom or love. If this is the case, I will teach you how to return to that feeling time and time again to help you revisit these feelings of euphoria to help you move forward in your grief journey and ultimately start to return to living your life forward.

Part Four

From the teaching of Neuro-Linguistic Programming (NLP), comes the concept of an anchor. The simplest way to explain an anchor is to think of it as a link to an emotional state. The anchor serves as a reminder or a trigger that puts you into a certain state of being. Of course, anchors can be both positive and negative; however, we're going to focus on positive anchors. For example, an athlete will use an anchor to get back into "the zone" so they can regain peak performance in a game. It may be a visual image of shooting the perfect basket or knocking the ball out of the park. A professional speaker will have a routine they do before going on stage to remind them of the positive states they want to be in while presenting. This routine is their way of setting up an anchor—or a positive state. You can use this same concept at any time to help you get out of a chaotic state of grief and revisit the feeling you felt in the previous exercise in order to try and continue your healing journey. Here's a guided visualisation to help you create your own anchor to a powerfully calm and peaceful emotional state—or any other positive state you'd like to access in times of stress. If you'd like to use a physical object as your anchor, be sure to have it with you at this time, or you can work with a visual image in your mind.

1. **Find a Comfortable Spot**: Choose a quiet place where you won't be disturbed for about 15-20 minutes. Sit comfortably, close your eyes, and take a few deep, calming breaths.

2. **Recall a Happy Memory**: Think of a memory that brings you joy or peace. It could be a moment shared with the person you're grieving, or it could be completely unrelated. The important thing is that this memory brings you feelings of happiness, comfort, and/or peace.

3. **Engage All Your Senses**: Immerse yourself in this memory. What do you see? What sounds are present? Are there any smells, tastes, or textures associated with it? The more detailed you can make this memory, the more immersive and comforting it will be.

4. **Create Your Anchor**: Choose a physical gesture or a phrase that can serve as your anchor. This could be a specific hand gesture, like touching your thumb and

middle finger together, or a comforting phrase, such as "peace resides within me".

5. **Associate the Anchor with Your Happy Memory**: As you continue to experience your happy memory, use your anchor. Make the gesture or say the phrase and let the positive feelings from your memory wash over you.

6. **Reinforce Your Anchor**: Continue to stay in your happy memory for a few more minutes, using your anchor repeatedly. Feel the connection between the anchor and the positive feelings growing stronger.

7. **Practice Using Your Anchor**: Gradually bring yourself back from the memory, keeping your eyes closed. Allow yourself to acknowledge the feelings of grief. Then, use your anchor. Perform your gesture or say your phrase and let the feelings of comfort and positivity from your happy memory return. Notice how the grief, while still present, becomes more manageable with the positive feelings alongside it.

8. **Repeat Regularly:** Practise this exercise regularly. Grief is not a linear process, and there may be moments of intense sadness even after a period of seeming improvement. Having this anchor can help provide comfort during those times.

Remember that life is what we make of it. How we perceive our environment is what creates our reality. If we look at life through the lens of negativity, then negativity is all that we'll see. If we choose to look at life through the lens of positivity, then we will see and experience positivity and be able to live in gratitude. It is a choice and, when we have tools—like the guided visualisation for anchoring a positive state—we can more easily and effortlessly navigate life's most challenging moments. This is where you will also begin to realise the power of the mind.

Final Thoughts

Some might say that this is the end game. The final stage of this roller coaster of a grief journey. What are you left with as you start to unravel the layers of pain, loss, guilt, anger, hurt, and frustration? Memories! Memories that can sustain you and hurt you all at the same time. Feelings that make your heart dance with joy and, at the same time, emotions that can feel like your past has slapped you in the face. Do we hold onto all the memories of the ones we have lost even when we know it is time to let go? If I am honest, there's comfort in that. There's comfort in staying in a familiar place, even if it hurts like hell. Using the exercises you have just done, I had unshackled myself from the chains of my pain only to replace them with the fear of moving forward. I knew I needed to create a new chapter of my life and let go of my grief, but there was more comfort in holding on to a past that no longer existed than there was stepping forward into an uncertain future that I was entirely unprepared for. The most fantastic thing about my relationship with Jesus is that His love has and does show me is a father's love. He never has and will never give up on me. Even when I can't, He already knows that I can. When I think that I will never be able to let go, He is already moving things in my life to position me for change. The only job I have is merely trusting that even if things make no sense to me at that moment, the love He has for me will never fail me. Holding on to the past was no longer an option. Jesus had designed my journey to get me to a place of being open and in a position of wanting to let go.

CHAPTER 11

MOVING FORWARD FEARLESSLY

HOW IT ALL BEGAN

A Danish philosopher and theologian, Søren Kierkegaard, quotes, "Life can only be understood backwards, but it must be lived forwards." As we have come to the end of our journey together, understanding how it started will hopefully make what you have read far more transformative for your journey. With that being said, I think it's critical to tell you how my relationship with Jesus started.

I was raised a Roman Catholic, so Jesus was not unfamiliar to me growing up. As a teenager, I ran away from all that was holy and lived a faithless adolescence. As an adult, I danced with my faith for many years. Dipping my toes in and out of believing and selecting with caution which parts of faith fitted best with my lifestyle.

Three days after my husband Benny passed away from a sudden asthma attack at 30, on April the 14th 2015. Amidst the chaos of those heartfelt but endless condolence phone calls; The kind and appreciated food parcels people delivered to our home—the looks of concern and love on my family and friends' faces of concern and love. In the middle of trying to breathe through the pain of how I would tell our then 4-year-old son that daddy would never be coming home, I experienced a moment of such clarity that I want to share with you. I can imagine you're thinking, how on earth could she have had clarity in a moment like that? Well, let me tell you, as I remember it as clear as day!

It had been three days since his death, and I decided to have a shower, wash my hair and try to make myself feel and look presentable. As I usually do when my spirits feel low, I put on music, and I sang to heal the dull ache that consumed my soul like a poisonous fungus. I sang in my bathroom for what seemed like hours. I was singing in worship to heal my pain and give thanks for the life and time that I had with this incredible human being. I felt like I was singing to save my life. Once I had finished, I stepped out of the shower and wiped the steam from the bathroom mirror. A memory came flooding back to me and hit my heart like an unexpected and unwelcome punch in the gut. My husband often wrote 'I Love You' on the mirror, but until the steam-filled up in the bathroom, I would never be able to see it. It always surprised me and made me smile. The memory moved from pain to filling my heart with gratitude for the small but powerful gestures he showed to make me feel precious and loved. But this time, there was no 'I Love You' staring back at me in this steam-filled mirror; it was only me. My reflection. The reflection of a different woman. The reflection of a widow, a single parent, and, most painfully, the reflection of being and feeling very alone. I stared at myself in that mirror for about thirty minutes. Reliving the last seven years of my life. Specifically, the events of the days leading up to kissing my husband goodbye for the last time. I recalled when we had our last conversation, and our final words to each other, which I'm so happy to say were, 'I love you, see you later.' There was a moment of clarity in this decisive moment of stillness with myself and my reflection. It was such an overwhelming moment of being present, a moment in which I was being 100% mindful as if seeing myself for the very first time in my 38 years of living. What I saw was a woman who had to make a choice, and right at that minute, Jesus spoke to me and said:

"Alisa, my most precious child. At this moment, right now, you have a decision to make! Now you can allow the devil to tell you that I don't exist. How could I have allowed this to happen to your husband? Why would I have taken him away from you and Jacob if I love you? If you decide to believe him, then your life, this journey, and that of your son's will be as dark as night. Or you can choose to 'follow me!' I can't promise you that it will all be easy. What I can guarantee is, it is going to be a painful road ahead. But what I can promise you is that I will take you from grief to glory, and your testimony will transform and save lives. I know you want to think this all through like you usually do, but you have no time. At this moment, right now, you have to decide."

And so, it began…… the day I decided to give my life to Christ. Jesus called me to go on a journey with Him, and what a journey He has and continues to take me on. On Saturday, October the 3rd, 2020, six months into the COVID 19 pandemic lockdown era, I was sitting alone on yet another evening, trying to stop my mind from wandering too far into the abyss of past memories, and when I decided to put pen to paper and start writing. I would be lying if I told you that I am #winning every day because that would be an out and out lie! Anyone who tells you that after losing someone, they are 100% healed is lying to themselves. While writing this book, there have been moments where taking myself back to the visual moments and recalling emotions has been so painful. Many times, I was in floods of tears from emotional exhaustion. The difference is that they are now only moments and not seasons of pain. Through Jesus's grace, I can move from that moment to a beautiful memory that makes me smile with ease. One thing I can tell you, though, is that Jesus kept the promise he made to me, which was that he would one day show me why Benny's death happened. He told me the journey would be painful, and as you have read my story, you can see that it was even worse than I could have envisaged. However, I trusted in His promise with all my heart, even when nothing made any sense. The times when I lost my way, he opened up new paths. He created new situations and brought people into my life to remind me to have faith. Six years later, I decided to write this book. It is a book that I knew I would write in June 2016 when the Lord first put the idea in my mind, and I placed it on my vision board* during my time in Barbados and believe me it's the first of many books that I will write to share my journey from grief to glory.

Vision Board 2016

Image above of my vision board from 2016. with an arrow my vision of becoming a number one New York times bestselling author.

Listen I am not here to try and convince you to become a believer in Christ, the sole purpose of this book is to give you hope. Hope that things can and will get better. Yes, it will take time and yes, the road travelled will be brutal. All I can do is share my story in all its fully faceted, complex glory. My story just so happens to be that Jesus was and is my hope for a better future. Because he created and formed me, he knows what he has planned for my life, both good and painful, he also knows the gifts, abilities, personality and heart he has shaped in me. I believe that all of these things have made it possible for me to travel from a place of grief to a new place of glory. When I look at myself and my life now, I can see the purpose of my pain. My assignment is to share my story with as many people as I can that are stuck in the season of sadness, the season of emptiness and the season of anger. People who are feeling or thinking that there is no way out of the darkness and that life will never be filled with light again.

Living Life Forward

For timeline's sake, I started to write this book in the middle of 2020. It feels like such a long time ago when we were all plunged into lockdown during the COVID-19 pandemic. Remember when we couldn't go out to see our friends and family? It was like we were all living in our own little bubbles. It was really hard not being able to hug the people we loved or do the things we normally would. But we found ways to stay connected, like video calls and virtual game nights. It wasn't the same, but it was better than nothing. Do you remember how people started getting creative with their hobbies and home workouts? It was like we all suddenly became chefs, bakers, and fitness gurus. And then there was the whole panic-buying situation. Remember how toilet paper and hand sanitizer were like gold dust? It was ridiculous, but at least it gave us something to laugh about and come together over.

But it wasn't all fun and games. Many people lost their jobs or had to work from home while juggling home-schooling their kids. It was stressful and took a toll on our mental health. But even then, we showed resilience and kindness, like when we started clapping for our NHS heroes every Thursday. Looking back, the UK lockdown during the

COVID-19 pandemic was a tough time, but it also brought us together in ways we never expected. We found new ways to connect, create, and care for each other. And now, as we move forward, let's hold onto that sense of community and compassion that got us through it all.

During that time I felt a sense of change within me. My period of metamorphosis was coming to a pivotal point just like the caterpillar's transformation within its cocoon. When a caterpillar undergoes metamorphosis, it transforms into a stunning butterfly or moth, unfolding its wings to soar freely in the sky. The process of metamorphosis is a true marvel of nature, consisting of several stages that culminate in a miraculous transformation. One could draw district parallels between the stages of grief and the metamorphosis of a butterfly.

The first stage of grief, similar to the caterpillar's retreat into its cocoon, is often characterised by shock and denial. The period where you feel numb or in disbelief about the situation that you had to face or may be now facing, and the struggle of coming to terms with the loss. The second stage of grief can be likened to the remarkable transformation that takes place within the cocoon. This is a period where we experience a range of intense emotions, such as anger, bargaining, and depression. Where you felt or may be feeling like the world is falling apart and that you will never be able to move forward.

Well I was finally feeling, like the butterfly or moth emerging from its cocoon, Slowly but surely, I was beginning to find hope and purpose again. I started to see life in a new way, with fresh eyes and a new perspective. I felt a new sense of independence and confidence; an enthusiasm to create new opportunities for myself, personally professionally and creatively. I was emerging from my grief cocoon as a changed person, with newfound strength and resilience. It was time for me to spread my wings and soar but this time with a more visible sense of clarity on where Jesus was leading the woman he had built me to be, and I was starting to feel free!

As my journey has evolved I am in a place of happiness that feels like constant sunshine on my face every day. That doesn't mean that every day is easy, but I am no longer living under a cloud of pain, loss, fear, dependency, addiction, depression, and all the other words and feelings associated with the grief and the traumas of my past. I know that it is time for me to step into my purpose and live a purpose-driven life, being able to introduce the incredible power of healing through my testimony. I decided to write this first book to tell people how Jesus has transformed my life through the tragic loss of my late husband. However, the true testament lies in what happened after my water baptism in April of 2019, where I was able to decode two decades full of deep-rooted psychological trauma that I can trace back to my single-digit childhood days.

Now I am making room for the new and am excited about what the 'new' will look like. The pain of the past will no longer cripple me. I no longer look at my past with rose-tinted glasses on, but I do look back and see that it's full of beautiful memories. My mission is to help and empower others, to give them hope that a bright new day is possible after a loss. My purpose is to share my story with women all over the world. I started a coaching movement to help empower other women to step through their looking glasses. Even if everything is the wrong way round, to begin with, I want them to see what a new world for them could look like on the other side of their reflection. If this is you, all you need to do is push past the fear of who the new you will be and start taking small steps forward. It is time to live with hope in your heart and take actionable steps to stop grief defining who you are.

I don't know if you have ever read the book 'Through the Looking Glass by Lewis Carroll. If you have not, then a quick overview: Alice climbs through a mirror into a fantasy world that she can see beyond it. There she finds that, like a reflection, everything is reversed. There are so many other dimensions to the book, but this is the basic overview. And so, like Alice, I decided it was time to step through my looking glass into a new world. This was the only way that I would see what was on the other side of my reflection. At first, everything was very jumbled up, and I felt like a new person in a foreign land. I had no idea what I was doing or where I was going, and I immediately knew that this would not be an easy walk. What I did know is that Jesus had not brought me this far to leave me stranded at the start of my new journey. Lewis Carroll ends his book with the line, "Life, what is it but a dream?" And he is right. Be brave. Be fearless. Dare to dream that you can and will find happiness again because you deserve it. Do not allow the grief cycle to engulf you like a tornado, damaging everything you encounter. It's time to let go of the past because the most damaging after-effects will always be to you. We cannot bring back the ones that we have lost, but we're still here. The best honour we can give is celebrating their lives through living and loving ours to the fullest.

I want you to do one final thing. Look at yourself in the mirror. Don't look at yourself; really SEE yourself! All the intricate details of your face. Your beauty and your flaws. Your perfection and imperfections. Your reflection will show you the pain of your loss and grief. But on this day, I challenge you to dare to dream about what is on the other side of your reflection! There **IS** a life that awaits you on the other side of the road you are travelling on and it's time to ask yourself this question out loud. 'The person that I love has died, but don't 'I' deserve to live?'

If you feel comfortable then I am going to bless you with a passage from the bible that is my favourite reminder that Jesus sees all of me because he created me. My hope is that it blesses you as you travel from your grief to your glory.

Psalm 139

1 You have searched me, Lord,
 and you know me.
2 You know when I sit and when I rise;
 you perceive my thoughts from afar.
3 You discern my going out and my lying down;
 you are familiar with all my ways.
4 Before a word is on my tongue

you, Lord, know it completely.
5 You hem me in behind and before,
  and you lay your hand upon me.
6 Such knowledge is too wonderful for me,
  too lofty for me to attain.

7 Where can I go from your Spirit?
  Where can I flee from your presence?
8 If I go up to the heavens, you are there;
  if I make my bed in the depths, you are there.
9 If I rise on the wings of the dawn,
  if I settle on the far side of the sea,
10 even there your hand will guide me,
  your right hand will hold me fast.
11 If I say, "Surely the darkness will hide me
  and the light become night around me,"
12 even the darkness will not be dark to you;
  the night will shine like the day,
  for darkness is as light to you.

13 For you created my inmost being;
  you knit me together in my mother's womb.
14 I praise you because I am fearfully and wonderfully made;
  your works are wonderful,
  I know that full well.
15 My frame was not hidden from you
  when I was made in the secret place,
  when I was woven together in the depths of the earth.
16 Your eyes saw my unformed body;
  all the days ordained for me were written in your book
  before one of them came to be.
17 How precious to me are your thoughts,[a] God!

How vast is the sum of them!
18 Were I to count them,
   they would outnumber the grains of sand—
   when I awake, I am still with you.

19 If only you, God, would slay the wicked!
   Away from me, you who are bloodthirsty!
20 They speak of you with evil intent;
   your adversaries misuse your name.
21 Do I not hate those who hate you, Lord,
   and abhor those who are in rebellion against you?
22 I have nothing but hatred for them;
   I count them my enemies.
23 Search me, God, and know my heart;
   test me and know my anxious thoughts.
24 See if there is any offensive way in me,
   and lead me in the way everlasting.

EPILOGUE

Every individual's journey through grief is uniquely personal, and wherever you find yourself along this path, I want to share with you five invaluable lessons that have profoundly impacted my own journey. While these lessons may not hold the key to resolving every hurt you may face, they are the truths I have discovered along the way. It is my heartfelt prayer that they bring you guidance, comfort, and hope in your own healing process. I also wanted to provide you with a section of the book that you can easily revisit and reference whenever you need it, a source of solace and encouragement in moments of need.

1. You Cannot Cheat the Process of Grief.
As much as I wanted to skip all the necessary stages of grief and fast track myself to the place I am at now, I would be doing you a disservice if I told you there is a shortcut to healing and that you can do x y & z to get to a place of glory. The simple truth that I hope you have realised is that, yes, there is a process whereby you have to physically, mentally and emotionally travel through grief. However, that road is unique to you. No one journey is the same, and you cannot

cheat your way through it. The only way to move forward is to take it one step at a time. Do not run or hide from the painful moments because of fear. If you don't face your fears and accept that it is an essential and integral part of the grief journey, it will do one of two things. It will either distract you or destroy you. For me, those distractions came in the form of dependencies and toxic habits, which, if I had left unchecked, I do not doubt would have led to the destruction of my life. Causing the snowballing of generational trauma, which could have had a life-changing impact on my son's life and his children's lives. And so, the circle of life would go on with ancestral chains bound together through the pain and hurt that started with the trauma and fear that I could not accept and move past. Overcoming the fear of moving forward is not something that I have been able to do in isolation, talking my pain out has been critical for my healing. I implore you, talk to people that you trust and, most importantly, talk to a specialist counsellor and therapist to help you decode what you're feeling and find your way through the eye of the storm.

Refer to chapter three on the process of grief and the importance of counselling.

2. Find Healthy Comfort Blankets

Find alternative forms of comfort that will help progress your healing, not prevent it. Numbing the pain with toxic habits can form dependency. It is essential to find healthy comfort blankets that make you feel alive, energised, positive and happy. I had three things that replaced alcohol, marijuana and sex. They were and remain constant positive influences on my continued growth. Writing is one, as I hope you can tell from this book.

Physical fitness is another. Yes, I want to look good and stay healthy, but the main reason I work out is to keep myself mentally fit. The challenge of lifting more weights or forcing myself to do one more rep enables me to train my mind and assists me in learning how to control my emotions. This is so important when trying to overcome any type of loss, trauma or issue in your life. Building and cultivating a resilient mindset is key to being able to move from grief to glory. This will be a crucial area of focus and teaching in my next book. And finally, to my greatest love of all outside of my son... Music. Music is such an essential part of my life. For every mood and for every moment, music is right there with me. Holding my hand when times are rough and being my dance partner in times of jubilation. In this season of my life, it was and remains my go-to. I want to say a personal thank you to the likes of Lecrae, Elevation Worship, Dante Bowe, Maverick City Music, Travis Green, Tasha Cobbs, and so many more. These songs have played an essential role in the development of my relationship with Jesus. Certain songs acted as the soundtrack to my healing and unjumbled the new year. These songs and many more decoded my fear. They continue to release a strength in my soul that gives me a burning desire to step further and further into my new season, a season of assured faith that everything will be okay and that the best is still yet to come.

Spend some time thinking about what healthy comfort blankets you can adopt to replace those toxic and unhealthy ones. Try not to overthink it. Just simply ask yourself - what things make my soul and spirit leap for joy? What makes me smile with all my being? When you know the answer, do more of it daily.

Refer to chapter nine and revisit the coaching exercises to help you let go of things that are stopping you from healing.

3. Be Transparent, Let People in And Unplug When You Need To

It is so easy to try and carry on with everything that life throws at you; even when the going gets really tough, we tend to try and keep going. I was always guilty of this. The pressure that came from me, to show everyone that I was a strong widow, was, in hindsight, a pressure that I need not have put on myself. Everyone around me knew I wasn't coping. A word of advice: people who know you the best can see through the smoke and mirrors and sometimes feel powerless to help you. What happened in my case was that because they saw me acting one way but sensing that all was not well, they hesitated to reach out to me to try and help. I, in turn, resented the fact that no one could see that I was pretending to be ok and so the cycle continued. This make-believe game, coupled with the psychological effects of grief, spiralled into a ball of depression which ultimately led to my breakdown. Internalising feelings of fear of how others may perceive your journey is not something you want to add to your list of burdens, so try and open up and let those you trust in. Easier said than done, I know. It is still; a work in progress even for me. I have learned to be more open and transparent about how I feel, the older and wiser I have become. Letting people know how I am feeling leaves no room for anyone to have to play guessing games. If I feel low, I send a message to my trusted circle, letting them know how and what I think; this gives them a fair warning that I am preparing to take some time out from life. I make sure I am crystal clear in what I need from them, so they know if I need their help or just need some time out to escape to my quiet place.

After having suffered from significant bouts of mental ill-health over the last couple of years outside of counselling, I have had to learn how to take time out and escape to my peaceful state of mind. It is vital to force myself to unplug from the matrix and think about nothing. This time of stillness gives me the ability to heal piece by piece. I spend time recalibrating my mind, body, and soul to think and see my life with more clarity. It may be as simple as turning my phone off for the day and listening to worship music with no outside distractions. Or asking my parents to have my son for a weekend to just have time out from doing mum things. I may take a half-day holiday from my job and head to a coffee shop by myself and people-watch in the afternoon. Suppose I need an intense period of introspection. In that case, I often take a social media detox and delete all my apps for a couple of months to spend that time focussing on my personal development. However large or small, my philosophy is based on making sure I am my whole self. To do that, I have to make time for myself, in short, prioritise time so that I can be my best self.

4. Don't Feel Guilty for Moving on With Your Life

I am going to keep this section short and simple. **Stop** feeling guilty for wanting to be happy. Life's for living not for continuously mourning the dead. It is so easy to get stuck in a place where you feel like every moment of joy you experience dishonours the memory of the person you lost. I had lost count of the times when I purposely made sure that I did not move my life forward for fear that people would look at me sideways. Possibly thinking, 'hmmmmmm, she couldn't have loved him that much if she can smile so soon after'. The only sincere piece of advice I can give you here is that to be frank, it is nobody else's business how you choose to heal and when you choose to move on with your life. That decision is yours and yours alone, never allow anyone to tell you otherwise.

The process of grief is complex enough, and I was hard enough on myself without adding other people's opinions to my list of woes. Guilt can cripple your growth and stifle your healing. It is natural to feel it but do not allow it to consume you, or you could remain in no man's land, never moving forward. I will return to the importance of my counselling here and the priority of finding routes to acceptance and closure - minus the guilt factor. Through counselling I learnt that I was being unfair to myself and the life I wanted to continue living. Also, knowing Benny as I did, the last thing he would want for me is a life without love and happiness. Ask yourself the question, what type of future would the person that you lost want for you? Then ask yourself, would you prefer to stay in pain out of loyalty to the person that has died, or do you deserve to live and be happy again?

Refer to chapter three on the process of grief and the importance of counselling.

5. The Power of Faith

This is not a hard sell to convert you to become a Christian, but rather a testament to the profound impact my faith has had on my life. Without it, I would not have survived, nor would I be living a purpose-driven life. Time and time again, the power of the Holy Spirit has shown up in my life, transforming it in unimaginable ways. With unwavering conviction, I decided to follow Him with every fibre of my being, and He has been faithful to His promises, guiding me on a remarkable journey from grief to glory.

My Personal Transformation

Let me share with you a pivotal moment in my spiritual journey. In April of 2019, four years after the loss of Benny and my decision to trust in Jesus, I made a public declaration of my faith through baptism. Baptism had not been a pressing need until I reached a point where I yearned to cleanse myself completely from the lingering darkness that seemed to shadow my existence. Although I believed I had moved forward, an invisible weight tugged at me persistently, a weight unrelated to grief. It felt like a deeper wound, buried and locked away. The night before my baptism, as I conversed with God in prayer, we both knew it was time to surrender it all to the water. I recognised that in order to embark fully on my purpose, I needed to break free from any chains that held me back.

On that significant day, with my loved ones gathered in my home church in Coventry, I felt an overwhelming readiness. There was no anxiety, only a deep conviction that everything was about to change. The main service had already been impactful, and as I retreated to the bathroom to change into my baptism clothes, I paused to reflect on the immense journey God had taken me on since 2015. He had carried me through the excruciating pain of Benny's passing, when my heart shattered into a million pieces. He had been with me through every stage of anger, depression, loneliness, and fear that followed. Instead of allowing grief to consume me, He helped me overcome my dependencies on destructive habits, such as sex, alcohol, and marijuana. In those moments when I believed I would never feel again, and when thoughts of ending my life seemed like the only escape from grief's clutches, God's presence was my solace.

Tears streaming down my face, I gazed at my reflection in the mirror, overwhelmed with indescribable gratitude. With a heart filled with gratitude, I offered a prayer:

"God, thank you for leading me to this moment. I am eternally grateful for the invaluable lessons you have taught me, preparing me for what lies ahead. On this day, I ask that it becomes a pivotal turning point where I surrender everything to the water. May my past truly become the past, washed away and cleansed anew. Break the chains of grief and fear, allowing me to step boldly into a new chapter of my life, free from apprehension. As I emerge from the water,

Lord, reveal anything that may consciously or subconsciously hinder my progress. Let nothing impede me from embracing the purpose you have ordained for my life. Today is the day, and the time is now. I am ready."

As I closed my eyes, I could sense a shift in the atmosphere, a profound sense of peace and anticipation for the transformation that awaited me. Little did I know, the journey was only beginning.

If you would like to watch a video of the special moment that was my water baptism, then head to my website justcallmealisa.com.

Embracing a Transformative Relationship with Jesus

After reading the powerful story of my personal journey, if you sense a readiness in your own heart to invite Jesus into your life and embark on a transformative relationship with Him, I invite you to join me in a simple prayer:

"Dear Jesus, as I reflect upon the incredible transformation you have brought into the life of Alisa, I am moved by the depth of your love and the power of your presence. I recognise that I, too, am in need of your saving grace and the guidance that only you can provide. I acknowledge that my thoughts, words, and actions have fallen short and have caused pain to others and myself. Today, I open my heart to you and invite you to come in and make me new.

Forgive me, Lord, for all the ways in which I have strayed and fallen short of your perfect will. Wash away my sins and cleanse me from the inside out. I surrender my past, my present, and my future to you. I desire to have a deep and

163

transformative relationship with you, where I can experience your love, grace, and wisdom in every aspect of my life.

Help me, Jesus, to follow you wholeheartedly, to listen to your voice, and to align my life with your teachings. Guide me in the path of righteousness and lead me into the purpose you have ordained for me. Fill me with your Holy Spirit, empowering me to live a life that glorifies you and brings hope and love to those around me.

Thank you, Jesus, for the sacrifice you made on the cross and for the gift of salvation. I am eternally grateful for your unfailing love and your constant presence. I surrender my life to you today, knowing that with you, all things are possible.

In your precious name, I pray. Amen."

As you utter this heartfelt prayer, may you feel the transformative power of Jesus entering your life, guiding you on the start of a remarkable journey of faith, purpose, and abundant life. Embrace the joy and fulfilment that comes from a deepening relationship with Him, knowing that He is always with you, leading you toward a future filled with hope and purpose. If you have sincerely prayed the prayer and poured out your heart to Jesus, know that He has heard you and lovingly calls you, His child.

As you embark on this transformative journey, I want to provide you with additional resources to support you along the way. Please visit my website, **justcallmealisa.com**, where you can download a complimentary e-booklet. This valuable resource will assist you in exploring the Christian faith, delving deeper into understanding who Jesus is, and discovering the profound significance of being His true followers. Through this e-booklet, you will find guidance, insights, and inspiration to nurture your growing relationship with Him. May it be a source of enlightenment and encouragement as you continue to walk hand in hand with Jesus, discovering the wonders of His love and grace.

ABOUT THE AUTHOR

Alisa's unconventional career journey has taken her from entry-level to executive leadership positions in eight countries across four continents, all without a university degree. At the height of her corporate career, tragedy **struck** in 2015 **and** Alisa's life took an unexpected turn. She found solace and purpose in her newfound Christian faith, which led her to pursue a career in ministry. Now the Director of Media for the Christian Broadcasting Network in the UK, Alisa combines her extensive global experience with her passion for serving others through ministry.

Through her coaching consultancy, justcallmealisa.com, she empowers young widows and women of all backgrounds to develop and embrace their multifaceted roles in society. Her inspiring story serves as a testament to the power of faith, resilience, and following one's heart to find purpose and joy in life.